Essential Irish
HISTORY
100 EVENTS THAT SHAPED IRELAND

Gill Books

Hume Avenue, Park West, Dublin 12

www.gillbooks.ie

Gill Books is an imprint of M.H. Gill & Co.

Copyright © Teapot Press Ltd 2025

ISBN: 978-1-8045-8197-1

This book was created and produced by Teapot Press Ltd

Text by Fiona Biggs
Designed by Tony Potter

Printed in Europe

This book is typeset in Futura and Optima

To the best of our knowledge, this book complies in full with
the requirements of the General Product Safety Regulation
(GPSR). For further information and help with any safety
queries, please contact us at productsafety@gill.ie

A CIP catalogue record for this book is available
from the British Library.

54321

Essential Irish
HISTORY
100 EVENTS THAT SHAPED IRELAND

Gill Books

CONTENTS

INTRODUCTION

From the end of the Ice Age to the dawn of the digital age, the small island of Ireland has had a complex history. It is a story of settlement and invasion, peace and conflict, poverty and prosperity, and oppression and sovereignty.

The prehistoric period, from around 7000 BCE, includes the Mesolithic and Neolithic ages, during which settlers arrived from mainland Europe and Britain. The new arrivals were hunter-gatherers and farmers, and the Neolithic inhabitants established a system of trade with neighbouring Britain. Their magnificent tombs, including those at Tara, Newgrange and Dowth, are a permanent reminder of their ingenuity and skill. The Celts, who would become the dominant cultural force, began to appear in 500 BCE. They brought tools and warfare, innovative farming practices and artwork and, importantly, the language that would eventually evolve into Irish Gaelic. With their distinct clans and chiefs and the druids who guarded their religion, this people would eventually give rise to the myths and legends of Ireland.

It is thought that Christianity came to Ireland around the beginning of the fifth century, before St Patrick arrived on his evangelising mission around 456 CE. He consolidated the religion in the country, adapting existing pagan practices and culture to the new belief system. Christianity heralded a golden age for Ireland. Monasteries became repositories of learning and art, and the country was renowned as 'the island of saints and scholars'. The valuable monastic artworks attracted the attention of the Vikings, who arrived on raiding missions from the end of the eighth century. They targeted the monasteries for their wealth, but soon, instead of pillaging and leaving, they began to stay, building permanent trading bases at Dublin, Limerick and Cork and importing new methods of farming and systems of

Brian Boru

local government. They formed alliances through marriage with the influential Irish families. Things came full circle when Irish kings began to attack wealthy Viking towns in much the same way as the Vikings had attacked the monasteries. The end of their era came at the Battle of Clontarf in 1014, when an army led by the High King of Ireland, Brian Boru, defeated a large Viking force.

The death of Brian Boru at Clontarf created a power vacuum, and the following century was one of violent conflict between the various kings. In 1171, Dermot MacMurrough, King of Leinster, asked King Henry II of England for help in settling a dispute with a rival. Henry sent Richard FitzGilbert de Clare, an Anglo-Norman nobleman known as Strongbow, who arrived in Waterford with a force of 1,200 men. With his help, Dermot recaptured his kingdom, and offered Strongbow his daughter's hand in marriage. When Dermot died, Strongbow took possession of his kingdom. King Henry then claimed Ireland and granted lordship over it to his son John, who later inherited the English crown. Ireland was lost to the native Irish. By the middle of the 13th century, more than three-quarters of the country was under the control of the Anglo-Normans, who called a parliament in 1264 to assert their dominance. A rebellion by the O'Neill clan of Ulster, initially successful, was later assisted by the arrival of an army from Scotland under the Bruces, in 1315. Famine intervened, the rebellion failed and the Scots went home.

In the mid-14th century the population, already weakened by famine, fell prey to the bubonic plague, the Black Death, which wiped out whole communities – it is estimated that a third of the population died. The English administration collapsed and Ireland reverted to lawlessness. In 1366 a parliament was called by the Duke of Clarence, one of the largest landowners, albeit absent, in the country. The parliament enacted the Statutes of Kilkenny, which prohibited inter-marriage and banned the speaking of the Irish language and the hiring of Irish soldiers. However, little changed in most of the country, and the English settlers, for their own safety, retreated to the eastern part of the country – today's counties Dublin, Meath, Kildare and Louth – to an area that became known as the 'English Pale'.

In 1477, England was distracted by the Wars of the Roses, and the most powerful man in Ireland, the Eighth Earl of Kildare, Garrett Mór FitzGerald, was appointed as the king's deputy in Ireland. He ruled until 1494, when King Henry VII, victor of the Wars of the Roses, sent Edward Poynings to replace him. The infamous 'Poynings' Law' clawed back power to the English monarch, who would henceforth have approval of all laws passed in an Irish parliament.

The Triumph of Death, Pieter Brueghel the Elder (1526/1530–1569). The painting reflects the social upheaval and terror that followed the plague, which devastated medieval Europe.

Introduction

When Gearóid Mór died in 1523, he was succeeded by his son, Garrett Óg, the Ninth Earl of Kildare. He, like his father, was appointed king's deputy, but refused to accept the status quo of Poynings' Law. He led a rebellion against the king, and was arrested and executed. The power of the Kildares was over.

The next development would have far-reaching consequences. By 1536, King Henry VIII was on the throne of England and had declared himself supreme head of the Church in England, breaking with the papacy. He did the same thing in Ireland and had himself recognised as king, rather than lord, of Ireland. Inside the Pale, the population toed the line; outside it, Catholicism thrived. Adherence to it soon became a symbol of defiance, a defiance that contained the germ of nationalism.

When Elizabeth I succeeded to the English throne in 1558, Ireland outside the Pale was out of the reach of the English administration. Lawlessness was widespread. A feud between the Earls of Ormond and Desmond in 1565 ended with Desmond being imprisoned by Elizabeth. His family rebelled against the crown and Desmond was released. In 1579 there was a second Desmond rebellion. This time Elizabeth sent in the troops. They laid waste to the Desmond lands in Munster, which were then settled with loyal Englishmen. At the dawn of the age of adventurers, Ireland was an opportunity for land-grabbers. By the end of the 16th century, the only part of the country outside the royal reach was Ulster, which was controlled by Hugh O'Neill, Earl of Tyrone. O'Neill was a constant thorn in Elizabeth's side, the instigator of ambushes and skirmishes. Elizabeth's initial attempts to match him failed, but when she sent a large army of 20,000 in 1601, O'Neill, bolstered by soldiers sent by Catholic Spain, was defeated at the Battle of Kinsale. Although the new English monarch, James I, pardoned the earl, the last vestiges of Irish power were gone, and the great Irish nobles of the north fled to the continent. Their land was confiscated and divided among Protestant settlers from England and Scotland, in what became known as the Ulster Plantation. It would have a lasting effect on the demography and politics of the region.

When Charles I succeeded James as king in 1625, he viewed Ireland as a ready source of revenue. His Irish deputy, Charles Wentworth, ruthlessly enforced the king's will, continuing with the policy of plantation and imposing new customs tariffs. He left in 1639 and a Puritan government was appointed. The Old English Catholics rebelled. When a show of force resulted in the exclusion of Catholics from the parliament, they formed a federation, known as the Confederation of Kilkenny, and rebelled against the English Protestants. Their rebellion took

place against the backdrop of the English Civil War, which ended with the execution of Charles I. He was replaced by a Lord Protector, Oliver Cromwell, who arrived in Ireland in 1649 at the beginning of a bloody campaign of suppression. By 1652 almost a third of the Catholic population was dead. Catholic tenants and landowners were pushed off their lands and forced to settle the infertile region of Connacht, and their lands were sold off to wealthy English to pay for the expenses associated with Cromwell's campaign. Some of the new landowners rarely set foot in the country. It was the beginning of the era of the absentee landlord. In 1666, Charles II was restored to the English throne. Some lands in Ireland were returned to their original owners and the country began to rebuild. In 1685, Charles was succeeded by his brother, James II, a devout Catholic. English religious sensibilities were outraged and a plan was hatched to import a Dutchman,

Introduction

William of Orange, James's son-in-law, to replace him as king. He arrived in England in 1688 and was crowned William III. James mustered Irish support, with the help of Louis XIV of France, but William invaded Ireland in 1690, at the head of a huge army. His victory over James at the Battle of the Boyne in July 1690 was decisive, although the war dragged on, finally ending with the Treaty of Limerick in 1691. Its terms were favourable to Catholics, and allowed soldiers loyal to James to leave Ireland, with their arms, prompting the departure from the country of the 'Wild Geese'. Despite the treaty, anti-Catholic laws were soon being enacted by the Irish parliament. Over a period of 30 years the 'Penal Laws' became progressively harsher. By the end of the first quarter of the 18th century almost three quarters of the Irish population was Catholic, but the power and wealth in the country were in the grip of the minority Protestant population.

The harsh winter of 1739 was the prelude to a two-year period of famine that would kill around a fifth of the island's population of 2.5 million. The famine resulted in a dependence on the potato as the main form of nourishment for the poor. However, in the wake of the famine, there was a relaxation of the Penal Laws and the population began to grow. Trade increased and a prosperous Catholic middle class emerged. Much of the revenue produced in the prospering country was claimed by the king, and the unfairness of this fanned the flames of an emerging Irish nationalism. In 1775, with the outbreak of the American War of Independence, British troops stationed in Ireland were withdrawn to fight in the American colony and the leader of the Irish Parliament, Henry Grattan, was permitted to raise a Protestant militia. The 40,000-strong Volunteers were supported by many Catholics, and when Britain lost the war in America, Grattan put pressure on the government to give Ireland legislative independence. The 20-year operation of Grattan's Parliament was a new era for politics in Ireland, and brought an economic boom. Rural rents soared, common land was enclosed for cattle grazing, and people fled to the cities, which soon became overcrowded. Those who stayed in the countryside formed secret and competing Protestant and Catholic societies and went on marauding sprees. The dominant Protestant group would eventually evolve into the Orange Order.

In 1792 the French Revolution began, striking fear into the heart of the British establishment. Grattan, together with a young lawyer, Theobald Wolfe Tone, founded the United Irishmen, which brought Protestants and Catholics together as a political force. After a positive meeting with the king and prime minister, Grattan put a vote to the Irish Parliament to repeal almost all of the remaining Penal Laws.

A later vote, in 1795, to repeal the last of those laws, was defeated, and the United Irishmen began to plot rebellion. Tone was promised help by France, but bad weather compelled a French expeditionary force to abandon their mission. The British rounded up the leaders of the aborted rebellion and Tone was sentenced to death. He cheated the executioner by killing himself in his cell. The government's draconian response to the plot swelled the ranks of the United Irishmen, and a badly organised rebellion took place in 1798, culminating in the doomed Battle of Vinegar Hill. Prime Minister William Pitt then proposed a union between the Irish and British Parliaments. The Act of Union was passed in 1800, against Grattan's opposition, and the Irish Parliament was disbanded. The situation remained tense and, in 1803, a revolt was plotted by the new leader of the United Irishmen, Robert Emmett. It went badly wrong, Emmett was

Introduction

arrested, sentenced to death and executed. In 1804, Grattan decided to continue his work for Catholic emancipation and took his seat in the Westminster parliament. He died in 1820, having come very close to achieving his aim. In 1823, a Catholic lawyer, Daniel O'Connell, founded the Catholic Association to promote full Catholic emancipation. In 1828 he won a seat in Parliament. In 1829 the Catholic Emancipation Act was passed, but then the minimum property requirement for voters in Ireland was raised to an unreasonable level, immediately disenfranchising 90 per cent of the Irish electorate. O'Connell, now leader of a group of over 40 Irish MPs, turned his attention to the repeal of the Act of Union. In 1838 he formed the Repeal Association, holding 'Monster Meetings' to promote the cause. In 1843 he was arrested on a spurious charge of conspiracy and spent three months in prison. Released in 1844, O'Connell reduced his demands

to the establishment of a separate Irish parliament that would deal exclusively with domestic issues. This capitulation cost him a great deal of support, but political concerns were soon overtaken by the most catastrophic event in Ireland's history.

In late 1845, the potatoes, on which around three million of the population now subsisted, were struck by blight. Prime Minister Robert Peel organised relief shipments of corn, which mitigated the effects of the disaster, but in 1847 the blight returned and Peel lost the election. With little political will to provide meaningful assistance, disaster turned into catastrophe. Starvation and disease were rife and emigration rocketed. Another blight in 1849 was followed by a massive outbreak of cholera. By 1850 a million people had died and a million had emigrated, mainly to America, a trend that would continue.

In 1858, the Irish Republican Brotherhood (IRB) was founded by James

Stephens, and supported by the Irish in the US. Its aim, the foundation of an Irish Republic, was far more ambitious than earlier attempts to gain partial independence from the crown. It had a limited impact at the time, but would go on to play a much larger role in the struggle for Irish independence.

In 1868, William Gladstone became prime minister of Britain. He would prove to be a good friend to Ireland in the struggle for Irish Home Rule that played out in the second half of the 19th century. He worked with Charles Stewart Parnell, but ultimately their efforts failed. Home Rule remained on the agenda into the early years of the 20th century. The John Redmond-led Irish Parliamentary Party, aided by a constitutional reform that weakened the veto of the House of Lords, eventually succeeded in pushing through a Home Rule bill in September 1914. The First World War had just begun and the legislation was temporarily suspended for the duration of the conflict. The Irish Volunteers, infiltrated by a radical arm of the IRB, marched in the streets demanding Home Rule. A rebellion began on 23 April 1916, Easter Sunday. The rising, like so many others before it, failed, but the brutality of the British response created martyrs of the condemned leaders and gave a new impetus to the fight for freedom. In the general election of 1918, Sinn Féin, founded in 1905, won 75 per cent of the vote, and instead of taking their seats at Westminster, assembled in Dublin in January 1919 in the first Dáil Éireann, declaring sovereignty over the whole island. The newly formed Irish Republican Army (IRA), the military wing of the self-declared Republic, led by Michael Collins, fought a war of independence that lasted from 1919 to 1921. The 1920 Government of Ireland Act divided Ireland into north and south, and the war ended in truce in 1921. The Anglo-Irish Treaty was signed in December of that year. It created the Irish Free State, comprising the 26 southern counties, to replace the Republic, making Ireland a dominion of the British Commonwealth of Nations. The outcome of the Treaty was a bloody civil war that lasted from 1922 to 1923, fought between the Free State government, led by Michael Collins, and the anti-Treaty IRA, led by Éamon de Valera. Cumann na nGaedheal, founded by William Cosgrave, won the 1923 general election and worked to establish a sound economic base for the country. De Valera, breaking with Sinn Féin in 1923, founded the Fianna Fáil party, an initiative that changed the face of Irish politics. In 1932, the Fianna Fáil party won 72 seats and with these de Valera was able to form a minority government. The Constitution of Ireland became law in 1937. It changed the name of the country to Éire, a sovereign and independent state. The 1948 Republic of Ireland Act created Ireland as a country outside the Commonwealth.

The new republic became caught in a downward spiral of economic stagnation and emigration. In 1959 Seán Lemass became taoiseach in a Fianna Fáil government and immediately set about setting up an industrial base for the country through investment from abroad. The economy started to grow and emigration dropped by around 65 per cent. The country's fortunes seemed to be on an upward trajectory, boosted in 1973 by Ireland's accession to the European Economic Community (EEC). After a time languishing in the economic doldrums in the 1980s, a period of unprecedented growth, known as the Celtic Tiger, prevailed from 1995 to 2007. The banking crisis of 2008 came as a sharp and painful interruption to the status quo, but the economy had started recovering by the end of 2012.

In 1969, Northern Ireland, which had opted to stay within the United Kingdom under the terms of the Anglo-Irish Treaty, erupted into violence born of anti-Catholic discrimination by the majority Protestant population. The situation escalated, British troops couldn't restore order and in 1972 the Westminster government imposed direct rule on the province as a stop-gap measure. The IRA then brought its bombing campaign to the British mainland. Efforts began in 1981 to come up with a lasting solution and in 1985 the Anglo-Irish Agreement was signed, providing for cooperation between the Irish and Northern Irish governments across security, legal affairs and cross-border cooperation. However, the violence continued. In 1994, the IRA, realising that their campaign would achieve nothing, agreed to lay down their arms. Four long years of negotiation culminated in the Belfast Agreement of 1998. The Republic agreed to give up its constitutional claim to sovereignty over the entire island, and the UK relinquished direct rule over Northern Ireland. Finally, a lasting solution was in sight, and a devolved legislature, the New Northern Ireland Assembly, met for the first time in July 1998. Although it has been suspended on several occasions, it sat for an unbroken period from 2007 to 2017, bringing a new stability to Northern Ireland.

From the second half of the 20th century, the Republic of Ireland has been transformed from a poor, inward-looking country, decimated by emigration and under the outsized influence of the Catholic Church, to a prosperous, socially liberal nation, confidently taking its place in the world. Northern Ireland, once so divided, has finally found a way to accommodate both its populations, and a whole generation there has grown up almost free of the sectarian violence that had so blighted the province.

Around 8000 BCE, the Ice Age was ending and rising seas caused by the melting ice sheets began to cut Ireland off from mainland Europe and Britain. The first settlers of the Mesolithic era, or Middle Stone Age, arrived by boat to an unpopulated, densely forested island. These hunter-gatherers ate berries and other wild plants, as well as fish, hare and birds. They also hunted larger animals like boar with rough flint-tipped spears. They were thus dependent for food on whatever was available in the wild. The earliest Mesolithic settlement in Ireland, dating from 7000–6500 BCE, was discovered at Mount Sandel in County Derry. Excavations uncovered the cooked bones of birds, wild pigs and freshwater fish.

People of the Neolithic era, or New Stone Age, arrived around 4000 BCE and gradually absorbed or displaced the Mesolithic people. They brought cows, pigs and sheep, seeds for planting grain crops, and the farming practice that had spread to Britain from the Middle East via Europe. They cleared land in the upland forests, planted crops, such as wheat and barley, and built

fortified villages. They ground their grain crops in handmills called querns and cooked their food in hand-thrown clay pots. When they discovered porcellanite in County Antrim, they began to mine it. This rock is much stronger than flint and therefore made excellent tools. Axe heads made from Antrim porcellanite have been excavated as far away as southern England, so it is clear that the Irish Neolithic farmers were trading with Neolithic Britons.

Neolithic tools were fashioned from flint or porcellanite, chipped into shape and polished with an abrasive rock.

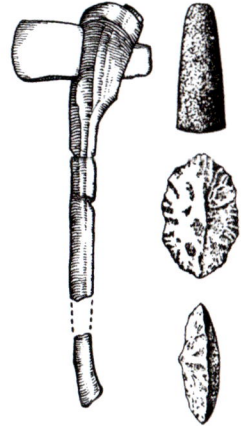

One of the oldest Neolithic field systems in Europe can be seen at the Céide Fields, near Ballycastle in County Mayo.

Although they left behind no stories or songs, Ireland's Stone Age settlers covered the island with hundreds of magnificent stone tombs. They left extraordinary monuments: great stone tombs for the dead, covered by mounds of earth. There were four kinds: court cairns, passage graves, portal tombs and wedge tombs.

The remains of over 1,000 Megalithic tombs can still be found in Ireland, particularly in the north. These tombs offer clues as to the lives and culture of the Stone Age people of Ireland. Court tombs are the oldest known form of Irish stone construction. They usually consist of a rectangular cairn constructed from dry stones.

Elsewhere, the settlers built passage tombs – long, rock-enclosed passages leading to a burial chamber. These passage tombs are of great significance as they contain early examples of Irish artwork. This was chiselled or carved into the walls of the tomb with sharpened rocks, and was often composed of geometric patterns such as circles, swirls, triangles or zigzags. Today, the meaning of this artwork can only be guessed.

The most spectacular passage graves are in County Meath – at Newgrange, Dowth and Knowth and on the Hill of Tara. Over a thousand years after the first tombs were constructed, people began building a third type: portal tombs. These usually have a single chamber, often covered with a gigantic capstone, and a pair of large portal stones form a doorway. How Stone Age people constructed tombs with stones weighing upwards of 150 tons is still a mystery.

The last variety of tomb built by the Stone Age Irish was the wedge tomb. This type of tomb first appeared around 2200 BCE, and construction carried on well into the Bronze Age. Between 500 and 550 wedge tombs survive, the largest of which can be found at Labbacallee, near Fermoy in County Cork.

Newgrange tomb near Drogheda was built in around 3200 BCE and is one of the best examples of a passage tomb.

In the early Iron Age, the Celts, the dominant power in western Europe, began a massive expansion that brought them to Ireland in several waves from around 500 BCE. They mixed with the existing population and eventually a language evolved that would become Irish Gaelic. Several hundred years later another group of Celts arrived from Britain, bringing with them iron tools and weaponry and an intricately patterned artwork, which was used to adorn jewellery and weaponry. Many of the detailed patterns of this artwork survive today in contemporary jewellery and design.

Like the Neolithic inhabitants of Ireland, the Celts were farmers. They settled in small groups based around the family unit, or clan. A warrior people, with superior weaponry, they took the best land for themselves, pushing the previous inhabitants into the rougher corners of the island and organising raiding parties to steal cattle and take slaves. The larger groups began to form kingdoms, and the kings led their armies against the other kingdoms.

In the clan system, everyone, from king or chief down to slave, knew his or her place. One group, the druids, the guardians of Celtic belief, existed outside of this strict hierarchy. The druids owed no allegiance to any chieftain or king and were able to move freely from clan to clan.

There were many gods in the early Irish world. The druids were the custodians of religious lore and they led the religious ceremonies. Some were soothsayers, believed to be able to predict the future, so people looked to them for advice and guidance. They also had a role as judges and as

By 400 CE there were five main centres of power – Ulster (Uladh), Leinster (Laighean), Munster (Mumhan), Connacht and Meath (an Mhí).

mediators in disputes. The coming of Christianity heralded their decline, although it was a gradual process. Eventually the druids became extinct, and because they kept no written records, all of their wisdom and knowledge were lost.

The Celts were farmers, living in small communities in about 150 small kingdoms.

Christian ideas spread slowly throughout Europe in the four centuries following the death of Jesus. In 431 CE, Pope Celestine I sent Palladius to Ireland as its first bishop. By that time many small Christian settlements already existed in the southern part of the island, and when St Patrick arrived on his evangelising mission in around 456 CE, he concentrated his efforts in the north. His church was well established by the time of his death, and he had appointed many bishops, who continued to lead the faithful. Within two centuries of his arrival, the whole country had converted to Christianity.

With Christianity came a new form of society, one centred on religion. The monasteries soon became the largest settlements in the country. Originally built of wood, they comprised a church and buildings for sleeping, eating and meeting. The main activities of the monks who populated them were praying, studying and producing food for the monastic community.

When the Western Roman Empire collapsed, a dark age spread through most of Europe. However, Ireland, thanks to the monasteries, experienced a huge surge in learning and art. Since Christianity came to Ireland peacefully, the Irish culture had had time to adapt to this new religion while keeping a sense of Gaelic individuality. The arts found new expression within the context of Christianity. Stone-carved Celtic crosses, intricate metalwork and glorious illuminated manuscripts were produced in the monasteries. For many, the age of the monasteries was the golden age of Ireland, when the expression of Gaelic culture reached its peak.

The larger monasteries became famous throughout Europe and were inevitably targeted by the Vikings for their wealth. It was, however, the Norman invasion of the 12th century that spelled the beginning of the end of the monasteries. The Normans built castles which soon became centres of local government and commerce. The wealth of the monasteries found its way to the great castles and the monastic artisans were soon working for the invaders.

An early Christian monastery reconstructed in the Irish National Heritage Park, Wexford, with a large Celtic cross in the foreground.

5 | 795–841 CE: The Vikings

The Vikings (the word means 'pirate') first came to Ireland in 795 CE. They travelled from Scandinavia in huge longships, and once they had landed, they attacked monasteries, killing and burning, and looting gold and treasure. For nearly 35 years they launched amphibious assaults all around the coast of Ireland, taking slaves and plunder back to Scandinavia. Initially, the raids were small and sporadic, and confined to the coastal areas, but around 830 CE the Vikings began to come in larger numbers, depositing their warriors on the coast at the mouths of the great rivers, equipped with small boats so that they could row into the interior of the country to sack the wealthy monasteries.

By the middle of the ninth century, the invaders were no longer plundering and departing, but staying to build permanent bases. Their fortified harbours were the first towns in Ireland, places of trade and commerce. Goods from all over Europe were soon being traded in Dublin, Limerick, Cork, Waterford and Wexford. Viking farming techniques were introduced and a form of local government was established for the first time.

By the end of the 10th century, the Vikings in Ireland had adopted Christianity and, under threat of attack from the Irish chieftains, had begun to intermarry strategically with noble Irish families. However, their power was on the wane. Although they still held several strategic towns, the great fleets were no longer sailing from Scandinavia to reinforce their numbers. The great wealth of their towns made them tempting targets for many of the Irish kings. Dublin was attacked by the King of Tara in 944 and the city was sacked.

In 1014, a huge army under the command of the King of Leinster, reinforced by a large contingent of Vikings, was defeated by King Brian Boru at the Battle of Clontarf, an event often regarded as marking the end of the Viking era in Ireland.

The Vikings came in longboat warships to plunder coastal areas.

In 997, after years of a power struggle, King Brian Boru of Munster and Máel Sechnaill II, High King of the Uí Néill clan, met and agreed to divide Ireland between them. Two years later they joined in battle to defeat Sitric, the king of the Viking settlement at Dublin. The alliance between the two Irish kings was not a natural one and, in 1002, Brian forced Máel Sechnaill to acknowledge him as High King of Ireland. For the next 10 years, Brian Boru travelled the length and breadth of the country, consolidating his position as lord of all Ireland. For a short period, Ireland came close to unity for the first time.

In 1013, Máel Mórda, King of Leinster, revolted against the High King and allied himself with Sitric. Brian rallied his forces and marched on Dublin where he was joined by Máel Sechnaill. For months they besieged the town, but failed to breach its walls. King Sitric used the time to send for help and Viking warriors were soon arriving from settlements in the British Isles and possibly beyond. Máel Sechnaill abandoned the siege, leaving Brian on his own.

On 23 April 1014, Máel Mórda led his Leinstermen and the Vikings onto a field at Clontarf, near Dublin, to face Brian Boru's assembled forces. The High King was by now old and weak and unable to fight, so his army was commanded by his son, Murchada. The battle raged for a full day, with many casualties, including Murchada and Máel Mórda. At sundown, the Viking ranks broke and they were routed. As one Viking fled the field, he stumbled across Brian's tent and split the old king's head open with his axe.

The death of Brian Boru was the beginning of his myth. His courage and determination have become legendary and his victory at Clontarf has come to symbolise the Irish spirit of resistance and sacrifice.

Battle of Clontarf, oil on canvas painting by Hugh Frazer, 1826.

After the death of Brian Boru, the political unity of Ireland dissolved and the country was plunged into a state of constant warfare between the local kings.

In the middle of the 12th century, Dermot MacMurrough became King of Leinster. In 1152 he kidnapped the wife of one of his rivals, Tigernán, King of Breifne. Although Tigernán's wife was returned unharmed, the King of Breifne held a grudge against his wife's abductor. Nearly 15 years later, he drove Dermot out of Leinster and out of Ireland.

Dermot appealed to King Henry II of England for assistance in recapturing his kingdom and Henry, in exchange for Dermot's allegiance, allowed him to recruit allies from among his Anglo-Norman nobility. Dermot recruited Richard FitzGilbert de Clare, known as Richard Strongbow, to his cause, together with a group of his kinsmen, the Geraldines.

Dermot returned to Ireland, recaptured his kingdom and offered Strongbow the hand of his daughter Aoife in marriage. Dermot and the Normans then marched on Dublin and captured the city. In 1171, Dermot died and Strongbow used his marital alliance to justify his taking control of the kingdom.

King Henry confirmed Richard de Clare as the Lord of Leinster, but claimed Dublin and some other territories for himself. He sent a vast expedition to Ireland on foot of a papal letter known as *Laudabiliter*, granting Henry the right to rule Ireland so that he could reform the Irish Church. When his army landed, many of the Irish kings submitted to him.

In 1185, Henry's youngest son, John, who had been granted lordship of Ireland, travelled to the country. He soon alienated most of the population

Dermot MacMurrough (1110–1171) abducted the wife of the King of Breifne.

by seizing land and giving it to his friends and allies.

When Henry died in 1189, he was succeeded by his eldest surviving son, Richard I. When Richard died in 1199, his brother John, Lord of Ireland, who at the time of his birth was very low on the list of succession, became King of England.

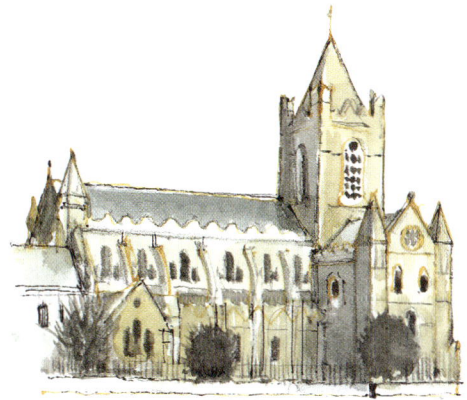

One of the first major buildings constructed by the Normans was Christ Church Cathedral in Dublin.

The Norman fortress of King John's castle in Limerick was built in the early 13th century.

The Normans saw Ireland as an opportunity to enrich themselves and they were soon arriving in the country in droves. By the mid-13th century, they controlled three quarters of the island. They introduced legislation that allowed individuals to own land – traditional Brehon law stipulated that land belonged to the whole family or tribe.

The Normans built castles, fortified existing towns and built new towns surrounded by stone walls in places like Athenry, Drogheda, Galway and New Ross. The only parts of Ireland that were not under Norman control by 1250 were western Ulster and parts of Connacht. The first Irish parliament met in 1264 at Kilkea Castle, near Castledermot in County Kildare. A symbol of Norman domination, the parliament was not yet an elected body and membership was confined to land-owning knights and jurors.

Brian O'Neill of Ulster attempted rebellion in 1258; a Norman army was defeated and John FitzThomas, Lord Desmond, was killed at the Battle of Callan in 1261. Domhnall O'Neill then called on Edward Bruce, the King of Scotland's brother, to take up the high kingship of Ireland, based on his own weak claim. In 1315 Edward brought an army from Scotland and quickly took control of Ulster and Connacht. Within a year he controlled Ireland north of Dublin. In 1316 he persuaded his brother King Robert to join him to complete his conquest, but by that time the country was being ravaged by famine. The army took food from the starving people to feed themselves and the Scots soon lost popular support. The Bruces retreated to the north and Robert returned to Scotland.

Edward regrouped and marched towards Dublin in 1318, but the Irish had lost confidence in the Scots, believing them to be worse than their Norman overlords. When Edward Bruce was killed at the Battle of Dundalk, the Annals of Ulster said that 'there was not done from the beginning of the world a deed that was better for the Men of Ireland'.

Edward Bruce

Kilkea Castle, site of the first Irish parliament, is a medieval stronghold
near the village of Kilkea, County Kildare. It is now a hotel.

In the mid-14th century, the bubonic plague (known as the Black Death because of the colour of the boils and pustules that grew on its victims) spread from the east across Europe, killing millions slowly and painfully. It was carried by the fleas that sucked the blood of infected rats; when the rats died the fleas found other hosts, preying on humans and passing on the disease.

Plague victims were gathered up before people became afraid to touch them.

Infected rats on merchant ships spread the Black Death along maritime trade routes. Dublin and Drogheda were two of the busiest ports in Ireland at this time, and it was here that the plague first arrived on rat-infested ships. From Waterford it was carried upriver to Kilkenny, Limerick and Cork, in some cases wiping out entire communities. It was so contagious that anyone who came in contact with the sick or the dead became infected. Bodies piled up, unburied, as people were afraid to touch them.

A Friar Clyn, of the Franciscan Friars Minor in Kilkenny, wrote: 'Many people In the world have died in such a short time of plague than has been heard of since the beginning of time … There was hardly a house in which only one died.'

By 1400 the population of Europe was half what it had been at the beginning of 1345, the year the Black Death first struck mainland Europe. It killed one third of the population of England and, although nobody counted the Irish dead, the death toll was probably about the same, putting the disaster on a similar scale to that of the Great Famine 500 years later.

In Ireland, the Black Death was concentrated mainly in the port towns and cities, affecting the Anglo-Norman population to a far greater extent than the rural Irish. Greatly weakened, they were vulnerable to attacks from the Irish. Trade came to a standstill, and the rulers of England, for a time, lost interest in their Irish colony.

Clerical victims of the plague, from the illustrated manuscript *Omne Bonum (Every Good Thing)* by James Le Palmer (c. 1320s – 1375), c. 1360–75.

King Edward III

By the beginning of the 14th century, Ireland was in a bad state. The Scottish invasion, plague and famine had laid waste to the land and the population. The country reverted to lawlessness. Absentee landowners were the biggest problem. The powerful English noblemen who owned large amounts of land in both Ireland and England generally preferred the ease of living on their English properties and paid scant attention to their Irish landholdings.

The most consequential absentee landowner was the Duke of Clarence, Earl of Ulster, the son of King Edward III. In 1361, Edward, concerned that the Anglo-Irish were putting their own interests ahead of the English monarchy, sent Clarence to Ireland as his lord lieutenant to reclaim his earldom from the Irish and to reinstate the royal authority in the country. A five-year campaign by Clarence achieved nothing. He pointed the finger of blame for his lack of success at the reluctance of the Anglo-Irish barons to help him. In a final attempt to assert the authority of the English monarch, Clarence summoned an English parliament in 1366, which passed the Statutes of Kilkenny.

The Statutes of Kilkenny were intended to return power to nobles who had been born in England, rather than their Irish-born descendants of several generations. The statutes had 36 prohibitions, and any breach was to be considered an act of treason, punishable by death. Among the 36 clauses in the statutes were draconian laws prohibiting the English from marrying the Irish, speaking the Irish language or employing Irish bards. Even the popular sport of hurling was outlawed, to be replaced by archery. The English could not adopt Irish children, use Irish names, wear Irish-style clothing, speak the Irish language, or play or listen to Irish music. They were even prohibited from riding a horse in the Irish fashion, without a saddle.

Unsurprisingly, given the weakness of the government in Ireland, the laws were unenforceable, but would later become a useful tool for the English monarchy to use against its Irish foes.

Lionel, Duke of Clarence

By the last quarter of the 14th century large areas of the country were completely under the control of Irish chieftains and the Anglo-Irish barons. The Anglo-Irish had assimilated over the centuries and had become more and more powerful. Richard II succeeded to the English throne in 1377 and came to Ireland twice in the 1390s in a last-ditch attempt to restore the power of the crown. Meanwhile the English colonists and settlers, who had been intended to consolidate the royal power in the country, decided to retreat to safety. By the 15th century, English authority extended only as far as Dublin, Kildare, Meath and Louth. The area was protected from attack by mainly wooden fortifications, and became known as the English Pale – deriving from the Latin word *palus*, a stake. In 1459 the Pale declared its independence from the crown, and in future the laws by which its inhabitants were governed would come exclusively from their own parliament.

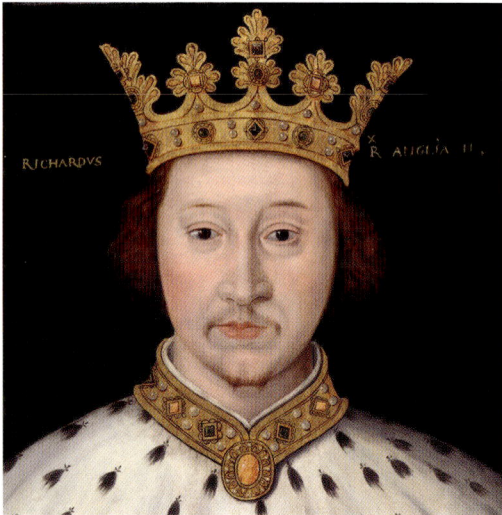

Richard II

The area of the Pale, represented in pink.

In 1488 an act of parliament defined the limits of the Pale, and in 1494 a rampart, 2 metres wide by 2 metres high, was built along an inner boundary to provide Dublin with a line of defence against Irish enemies and English rebels (the remains of parts of this rampart can still be seen today). Confined within the Pale, the English stood on the edge of crisis. Speaking English and adhering to English customs, they were nevertheless unsupported by the English crown, and a concerted effort by the Irish could have wiped them out very easily. However, caught up in their endless feuds, the native Irish were unable to organise themselves for that final blow. Their failure would eventually cost them their freedom.

The Pale dwellers considered themselves superior to those who lived 'beyond the Pale'. That sense of superiority was blown away in the mid-17th century by Oliver Cromwell, who made no distinction between those inside and outside the confines of the Pale.

Remains of the Pale ditch at Kilcross, County Dublin.

As the second half of the 15th century dawned over Ireland, the people of the island remained divided into their three distinct social groups. Although these were not necessarily political distinctions – groups from different societies often allied with one another – the divide between the groups remained an impediment to the unification of Ireland. This changed with the rise to power of the Earls of Kildare.

The Earls of Kildare were a Welsh Norman family descended from the Geraldines, a noble dynasty with its origins in Tuscany, Italy. They came to Ireland in the first wave of Normans that invaded the country in the second half of the 12th century. Their descendants, like most of the Anglo-Irish population, adopted many native Irish customs and practices in the centuries that followed. They made alliances with the Irish chieftains to consolidate their power, and they intermarried with influential Irish families.

In 1478, while England was focused on the War of the Roses, Garrett Mór (Gerald) FitzGerald succeeded to the earldom of Kildare. The Eighth Earl of Kildare would soon gain a reputation as the 'Great Earl' among the Irish and the English inhabitants of the Pale. A master politician, gifted with diplomacy, he was well placed to win support from all the inhabitants of Ireland. In 1477 King Edward IV, realising that he could be a unifying force, appointed him his deputy in Ireland. For nearly 20 years, as lord deputy, Kildare was king of Ireland in all but name. Even though he supported some failed rebellions against the English crown, he was always pardoned because of his power and his usefulness to the monarch. For the first time since the days of Brian Boru, Ireland enjoyed a semblance of peace and unity. The Great Earl's sway, however, would diminish after the War of the Roses, when Henry VII, the first monarch of the Tudor dynasty, was crowned King of England.

Gerald FitzGerald, 14th Earl of Desmond, leaves via Lough Swilly for France, c.1575 (J.C. McRae after H. Warren, 1884).

By 1485, the War of the Roses had reached a conclusion, and the first of the Tudor monarchs, Henry VII, had ascended the English throne. Without the distraction of war, Henry was able to focus on Ireland. He decided to send Sir Edward Poynings to Ireland in 1494 to replace Kildare as lord deputy and return control of Ireland to the throne.

Poynings arrested Kildare and immediately called a parliament. It drew up a document known as Poynings' Law, stating that all legislation proposed by the Irish parliament would henceforth have to be approved by the King of England. Henry then recalled Poynings and released Kildare. Realising that keeping the peace in Ireland depended on the earl, he reinstated him as his deputy. Kildare was now no more than a figurehead, the real power residing with the English crown, which was inherited in 1509 by Henry VIII.

In 1523, Kildare died, leaving the earldom to his son, Garrett Óg, who concentrated his energies on acquiring more Kildare family landholdings. Henry appointed him lord deputy, like his father, but Garrett Óg lacked his father's diplomacy and

A 1530 portrait of Gearóid Óg FitzGerald, Ninth Earl of Kildare.

came into constant conflict with the crown. He was appointed deputy no fewer than three times, and was then arrested on three occasions for various political reasons. When Garrett Óg was imprisoned in the Tower of London, he handed over the running of the earldom to his son, Lord Offaly.

Lord Offaly had the nickname 'Silken Thomas', a reference to his fancy clothing. In 1534, after his father's arrest, he rode to the Irish Parliament to renounce his allegiance to the king, then led his men on a rampage through the English Pale. During this impromptu rebellion, his men happened upon the Archbishop of Dublin, John Alen, and murdered him. Silken Thomas was excommunicated for this heinous crime, as a result of which support for him melted away. He was arrested and executed and his title was forfeited.

The powerful Kildare dynasty had been toppled, and Ireland was now a possession of the English crown.

'Silken Thomas' and five of his uncles were beheaded at the Tower of London in 1537.

With the influence of the Kildares gone, Henry VIII decided to extend his control in Ireland by creating a Church of Ireland. A parliament in Dublin in 1536 called for the dissolution of the Irish monasteries and the recognition of Henry as the head of the Church of Ireland.

The English nobility and the senior churchmen who sat in parliament had always envied the great wealth of the monasteries and, as in England, viewed their dissolution as an opportunity to acquire valuable landholdings. Without any powerful dissenting voices, the resolution passed, and the ancient monasteries were destroyed. The parliament then moved on to the creation of a Protestant Church of Ireland.

Since the days of King John, the English monarch had had the title Lord of Ireland. In 1540, Henry VIII's deputy in Ireland, Sir Anthony St Leger, called another parliament and pushed through a bill declaring Henry to be King of Ireland. Henry VIII's authority in all matters of religion and state was now unassailable. This change created divisions along the lines of religious and national identity that still haunt Ireland and Britain.

Portrait of Henry VIII by Hans Holbein the Younger.

Powle del. V.Green, Vigorniensis e sculptoribus regiæ Majestatis Æri incisit
Sir John Perrott,
Deputy of IRELAND.
Published Jan. 1, 1776.

Sir John Perrot (1527–1592), said to be a son of King Henry VIII, soldier and Lord Deputy of Ireland.

Henry's area of interest was confined to the English Pale. Outside of it, the Catholic Church increased in strength and influence. The monks who had been forced from their monasteries and those priests who had remained loyal to the Church in Rome preached the authority of the Catholic Church. The Irish and many of the Anglo-Irish defiantly confirmed their allegiance to the Roman Church. They took their children out of English schools and sent them abroad to attend Catholic schools in Europe. A new generation of Irish found vocations to the priesthood, focused on keeping the flame of the Catholic faith burning in Ireland.

While the royal writ held sway in the English Pale, the rest of Ireland came under the control of individual barons and chieftains. Lawlessness prevailed, with cattle-raids, skirmishing and assassination commonplace.

In 1565, there was a battle at Affane, County Waterford, between the 15th Earl of Desmond and the Earl of Ormond. During the battle, Ormonde's brother, Sir Edmund Butler of Cloughgrenan, shot Desmond in the right hip with a pistol, cracking his thigh bone and throwing him from his horse. He survived, but Queen Elizabeth I, who had succeeded to the throne in 1558, summoned both earls to England. She released Ormond, but imprisoned Desmond in the Tower of London. Desmond's cousin, James FitzMaurice FitzGerald, organised an uprising against the crown. Although limited mostly to the area of Munster, the rebellion ran for several years, eventually running out of steam when Desmond was released and FitzMaurice went into exile.

In 1579, FitzMaurice returned to Ireland with a small band of supporters and proclaimed a holy war against Elizabeth, who had been excommunicated by the pope. Although

FitzMaurice was killed soon afterwards, others continued the fight. The Earl of Desmond was one of them. Elizabeth took a more direct approach to this rebellion, sending a small army to Ireland to quell it. Her soldiers engaged in a scorched-earth policy, burning crops and slaughtering livestock. All men of military age were deemed traitors and liable to be executed. Tens of thousands of people died of starvation. By the time Desmond was killed and the English army had prevailed, Munster had been devastated.

Elizabeth confiscated huge tracts of land and instigated the Munster Plantation, giving English settlers a certain number of acres of land in return for rent to the crown. The plantation, poorly organised and rife with corruption, largely failed, and much of the confiscated land eventually reverted to its original owners.

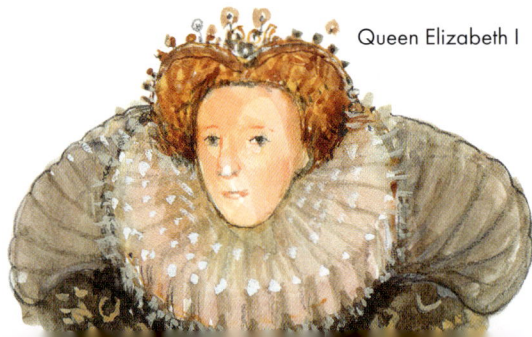

Queen Elizabeth I

The death of Gerald FitzGerald, 15th Earl of Desmond.

Trinity College was founded in 1592 by a small group of Dublin citizens who had received a royal charter to set up Ireland's first university. Elizabeth I saw it as an opportunity to consolidate Tudor rule in Ireland. The college was modelled on the universities of Oxford and Cambridge. During the first 50 years of its establishment it received large endowments and bought more land. Books were acquired that laid the foundation for what is now the largest library in Ireland. Its most famous acquisition is the Book of Kells.

Though Trinity was regarded as the university of a Protestant elite, Catholics were admitted from its foundation. However, the conditions that were imposed until 1793 made it difficult for them to graduate, and there were several other restrictions that were not lifted until 1873. As a result, Trinity was viewed as the university of the Protestant ascendancy. In 1871, concerned that it was being made easier for Catholics to attend what they regarded as a Protestant institution, the Catholic hierarchy issued a ban on their attendance, which subsisted until 1956, and was enforced, with few exceptions, by the Archbishop of Dublin, John Charles McQuaid, until 1970. The first Catholic provost was elected in 1991.

Women were admitted to Trinity in 1904, and the first female provost was elected in 2021.

Over the centuries the alumni of Trinity College have contributed greatly to the intellectual, scientific and literary life of the country. Some of the most influential Irishmen of the 18th century, including Jonathan Swift, Oliver Goldsmith, Edmund Burke, Henry Grattan and Wolfe Tone

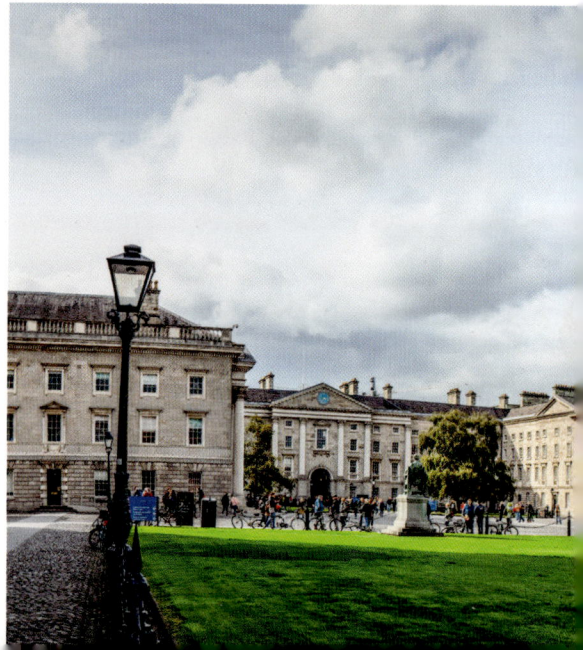

graduated from the college, as did four holders of the office of President of Ireland: Douglas Hyde, Éamon de Valera, Mary Robinson and Mary McAleese. Other notable alumni include recipients of the Nobel Prize George Bernard Shaw, Samuel Beckett and William C. Campbell, playwright and poet Oscar Wilde, and actor, comedian and screenwriter Aisling Bea.

Trinity College Dublin

Hugh O'Neill (c.1540–1616), 2nd Earl of Tyrone

During Elizabeth I's reign, royal control extended over more of Ireland. Increasing numbers of Irish chieftains submitted to the crown, and the English administration in the Pale became more self-sufficient. Ireland began to provide Elizabeth with regular revenue, and once again the English began coming to the country to lay claim to valuable parcels of land. By the end of the 16th century, the only region that remained outside royal control was Ulster, which was effectively ruled by Hugh O'Neill, the Earl of Tyrone.

In 1593, tensions between the Ulster Irish and the English land-grabbers turned into open conflict. It was the beginning of the Nine Years' War. Hugh O'Neill had been biding his time, making a good pretence of of being loyal to the crown, while masterminding an uprising. In 1594 he dropped the pretence and set his army on the English. An excellent tactical commander, he lured the English forces into ambushes and defeated them easily. He would then parley for peace so that he could regroup and redeploy his men.

Elizabeth commissioned the Earl of Essex to lead a large army to Ireland to deal with O'Neill. When his campaign failed, Elizabeth sent a second, much larger army.

When the Spaniards landed in Kinsale, they were besieged by the English army.

O'Neill had worked in secret for years to form an alliance with the Catholic Spanish monarch. In September 1601, 4,000 Spanish soldiers landed at Kinsale, hundreds of miles from O'Neill's power base. He marched his army southwards and, for the first time, met the English in an open battle on 24 December. Vastly outnumbered, his army was quickly defeated. In the aftermath of the battle O'Neill eluded capture, conducting a guerrilla war while the English pursued a scorched-earth policy. Elizabeth's successor, James I, pardoned O'Neill and allowed him to retain his earldom. But the power of the Irish was broken and soon their last great chieftains would flee the island. With all effective opposition gone, the new English king's power over Ireland seemed to be copper-fastened.

Although the great Irish lords of the north had been defeated by the military might of England in the Nine Years' War, they had managed to hold on to much of their land and power. Then, on 4 September 1607, they unexpectedly boarded a ship at Rathmullen and set sail for Spain. Although they took with them as many members of their families as they could gather, O'Neill left behind a son and Hugh O'Donnell, Lord of Tyrconnell, abandoned his pregnant wife.

Why did they leave? There are various theories, ranging from a plot with Spain that was discovered to information about a possible assassination plot by the English lords in Ireland. Either is possible, but nobody knows the real reason for their departure. The ship carrying the earls never reached Spain. High winds blew it off course, and it found safe harbour in Normandy, giving rise to a serious diplomatic incident between England, France and Spain. France refused to extradite the fugitives to England and Spain professed ignorance of the entire affair. Eventually, the earls were given safe passage to Rome, where they quietly lived out the remainder of their lives.

The Flight of the Earls is often depicted romantically as a final defiant act against the English, but it is more likely to have been a desperate act of self-preservation. Their sudden departure was a total disaster for the Irish they left behind in Ulster. King James declared the earls and their companions traitors and their lands, amounting to almost 500,000 acres, became forfeit to the crown. The English government displaced large sections of the population, and parcelled out small pieces of the confiscated land to settlers from England and Scotland, in an initiative that became known as the Ulster Plantation.

A depiction of Irish nobleman Red Hugh O'Donnell in the Kevin Barry Memorial Window in UCD Belfield, by Harry Clarke Studios.

Ultimately, the Ulster Plantation can be seen as a partial success for the English. The Flight of the Earls had dampened the region's tendency towards rebellion and the new settlements were a cost-effective way for a cash-strapped English monarch to ensure a friendly population in Ulster. Unfortunately, the plantation set Protestants and Catholics at odds with each other and would be the main contributor to the island's eventual partition. The incoming settlers, drawn from every class in British society, viewed the Irish as enemies, and even the Old English were at risk of having their land taken by the newcomers.

Previous plantations had been attempted in Ireland, including Mary Tudor's plantation of the midlands in the mid-16th century, and the Munster plantation of 1585 in response to the Desmond Rebellions. However, those earlier plantations had had none of the huge ambition of the Ulster Plantation, in terms of both size and efficiency. The land was split into lots of 1,000–2,000 acres and put up for rent, but the playing field was not level. The English settlers had first choice, and were allocated the best land and the lowest rents; part of the deal was that they had to settle a certain number of English families. The Scottish were also

Irish tenants were expected to pay exhorbitant rents.

offered good land at reasonable rents. The Irish got the leftovers, about a fifth of the landholdings on offer, at vastly inflated rents, and only for the lifetime of the tenant.

From the outset, there were problems. Despite the favourable terms and conditions, it proved impossible to recruit enough people to settle the available land and the settlers therefore had to employ Irish workers illegally. Some settlers decided to take the profit from the land from the comfort of their homes on the mainland. The huge rents demanded of Irish tenants forced many of them away from the land and into the forests, where they lived as outlaws. Already, there were two distinct populations.

Arthur Chichester, Lord Deputy of Ireland, one of the main planners of the Ulster Plantation.

Thomas Wentworth,
First Earl of Strafford,
after Anthony van Dyck
(1599–1641).

When Charles I succeeded to the throne of Britain and Ireland in 1625, he was in need of money to fund an ongoing war with Spain. Ireland, again, looked like a good fundraising opportunity. At that time the Old English were seeking 'Graces' from the king so that their rights would be protected. They wanted to guarantee their property rights, have the Oath of Supremacy repealed so that they could participate at the highest levels of society and have the recusancy fines for not conforming to the Established Church abolished.

Charles, hinting (but not promising) that he would guarantee the Graces, raised the huge sum of £120,000 from the Irish. He then sent Thomas Wentworth to Ireland as his deputy. Wentworth arrived in Ireland in 1632 and embarked on what he called a 'thorough' reform of the administration there. He established new customs duties and included Ireland in the lucrative trans-Atlantic trade that had come about as a result of the colonisation of America. He seized parcels of land based on old royal claims and put it up for rent. His zeal and dictatorial approach made him known as 'Black Tom Tyrant'.

In England and Scotland, Charles I was also trying to browbeat the population into submission, an attempt to gain absolute power that led to the English Civil War. Wentworth left Ireland with an army to fight for the king, but not before forcing the Scots settlers in Ireland to take the 'Black Oath', breaking their religious connection with Scotland.

Black Tom's loyalty went unrewarded. England had split into factions and he was arrested by the anti-royalists in the English Parliament on charges of subverting the laws of England and Ireland. His many enemies had their day in court. Despite his unswerving loyalty to his king, Charles I didn't have the courage to support him and had him executed in 1641.

Thomas Wentworth's departure from Ireland in 1639 left an enormous power vacuum. The weak Puritan government that was appointed in Ireland exacerbated the situation. The Catholic Old English landowners, who had never been granted their Graces, began to plot rebellion.

In 1641, a group of Old English in Ulster formulated a plan to take over Dublin Castle, the centre of the English administration. The plot was betrayed, but the rebellion went ahead and had soon spiralled out of control. With attention focused elsewhere, the native Irish in Ulster attacked their English landlords. Thousands of settlers were murdered and thousands more fled to the towns.

By 1642, the rising had spread from Ulster until almost the entire country was involved. Lurid stories of murder and massacre forced the government in England to take action. A small Scottish army arrived in Ulster to beat the rebels into submission. English troops were sent to Dublin, and Catholics were banned from attending the Irish Parliament. Many formerly loyal Old English Catholic landowners, thus disenfranchised, sided with the rebels. They met in Kilkenny and formed the Confederate Catholics of Ireland. For the next 10 years, this organisation functioned as the de facto government for most of the island outside the Pale.

The Confederate War turned into a rebellion of Irish Catholics against English Protestants, under the command of the Earl of Ormond. As the war raged in Ireland, the Civil War broke out

Václav Hollar's engraving of supposed atrocities committed by Irish Catholics during the rebellion of 1641.

in England. The loyalties of the English Protestants were divided between the Royalists and the Parliamentarians, while some of the Irish supported the Royalists and others were loyal to the Roman Catholic Church.

The war in England ended with the execution of Charles I in January 1649. In August of that year, a new army landed in Ireland. Oliver Cromwell, one of the leaders of the Parliamentarian army during the Civil War, was at its head.

Bunratty Castle, besieged by the Irish Confederates and taken from an English Parliamentarian force in 1646.

When he arrived in Ireland, Cromwell acted quickly to prevent an alliance between the Royalists and the Irish. He marched his army to Drogheda, and when it refused to surrender, laid siege to the fortress town for seven days. Then his heavy artillery breached the walls and his troops rampaged through the town, killing everyone they came across. Up to 3,500 people died.

Drogheda was the example Cromwell had hoped it would be, and most Irish towns surrendered and were left unharmed. However, while the negotiations for a surrender were still under way at Wexford, soldiers stormed into the town and murdered nearly 2,000 people.

By 1652 almost a third of Ireland's Catholic population had died in the fighting or of the plague and famine that accompanied it. Cromwell's victory, however, came at a huge financial cost to an administration whose finances were already depleted by the Civil War. Parliament now owed £3.5 million to investors, money-lenders and soldiers. They looked to Irish land as a means of raising the revenue.

In 1652, the English Parliament passed the Act of Settlement. English soldiers roamed the Irish countryside, arresting traitors and either executing them or forcing them to leave their lands and go to Connacht. Forced out before the harvest, and weakened by hunger on the long march westwards, the dispossessed Irish arrived in Connacht too late for crop planting. Almost all of the old Catholic landowners were exiled to Connacht and wealthy English took over their properties. The idea of an Irish landholding didn't appeal greatly to the lower classes – more than 30,000 English soldiers were given grants of Irish land, but 20,000 of them sold their holdings to their officers or other wealthy English.

A new class of rich Protestant English landowners could now lord it over an oppressed Catholic minority. The English government had meddled in the country's demographics to the extent that Ireland became a byword for societal inequality and instability.

In September 1649 Cromwell besieged Drogheda, slaughtering nearly 3,500 soldiers, women and children, calling it 'a righteous judgement of God'. In October, his army did much the same at Wexford. At least 2,000 were killed in Wexford, and those not killed in Drogheda and Wexford were sent to Barbados as slaves.

The restoration of Charles II to the English throne in 1660 brought a degree of peace to Ireland. Some of the harsher Puritan laws were repealed and the king returned some of the lands that had been taken from Catholics. The Earl of Ormond was appointed as his deputy in Ireland, and the stability of the next 25 years gave the country some breathing space in which to rebuild. Charles died without an heir in 1685, and was succeeded by his Catholic brother James. When Richard Talbot was appointed as the king's deputy in Ireland he purged the army in Ireland of Protestants, ensuring its loyalty to James Stuart.

In 1686 James's English subjects, disliking his Catholicism, began plotting to replace him with his son-in-law, the Protestant Prince William of Orange. In 1688, William landed in Devon, and had soon been crowned King William III. James fled to France, where Louis XIV seized the opportunity to challenge his old enemy, the Prince of Orange.

Louis provided James with a small army and sent him to Ireland. On 12 March 1689, James landed at Kinsale with his Jacobite army. Derry and Enniskillen supported William, so James

The Battle of the Boyne,
Jan Wyck, 1644–1702.

marched to Derry with 30,000 soldiers and demanded its surrender. The city withstood the siege for 15 weeks, until an English fleet fought its way through to relieve it. James retreated south, towards Dublin.

In June 1690, William, an experienced military commander, led an army of 30,000 men into northern Ireland. He marched in the direction of Dublin, and was as joined by 1,000 Irish troops en route. James and his 25,000-strong Jacobite army took a stand alongside the River Boyne, a few miles outside Drogheda.

The battle, which deployed the largest number of troops ever on an Irish battlefield, began on 1 July 1690. James was completely out-manoeuvred by William and soon retreated. After the battle, William went on to take Dublin and James once again fled to France. The Jacobite cause was dead in the water.

After their defeat at the Battle of the Boyne and James's departure to France, Ireland's Catholics continued the war in the hope of regaining their own freedom and land. They held on for more than a year, desperately trying to stop the slow advance of the English army. In July 1691, they were routed at the Battle of Aughrim, in Galway, the bloodiest battle in Ireland's history.

With the Jacobite cause in its death throes, command passed from the dying Richard Talbot to Patrick Sarsfield, Earl of Lucan. Sarsfield gathered his remaining forces at Limerick, and put up such a brave defence that the English army was convinced that the city couldn't be taken. The two sides agreed to parley and the war ended on 3 October 1691 with the signing of the Treaty of Limerick.

Patrick Sarsfield, Earl of Lucan (d.1693), Unknown Artist, England, 17th century.

The treaty granted Catholics the religious freedom that they had enjoyed during the reign of King Charles II and they were also given a guarantee of protection from prosecution for treason or other crimes related to the war. Jacobite soldiers were guaranteed free passage out of Ireland with their arms, if they wished to leave the country. Twelve thousand took advantage of this offer; the 'Wild Geese' flew from Ireland, never to return.

King William, a tolerant man, believed that the terms of the treaty were fair and was glad to see an end to the war. The parliaments of England and Ireland took a different view. Within five years of the signing of the treaty, the Irish Parliament began once again to pass laws that discriminated against Catholics. To the disillusioned Irish, the Treaty of Limerick became known as the 'Broken Treaty'. In 1702 King William died and the English monarchy passed to his hardline sister-in-law, Anne.

Irish Jacobite troops leaving Limerick for France, an exodus known as the Flight of the Wild Geese, following the Treaty of Limerick, 3 October 1691. Women with children attempted to join them, some drowning.

For 30 years after they first started ignoring the terms of the Treaty of Limerick, the Irish Parliament continued to legislate against Catholics, the laws becoming increasingly stricter. Collectively known as the 'Penal Laws', they barred Catholics from sitting in Parliament and from serving as sheriffs or as members of a town council. They couldn't join the army, own a gun or become lawyers. They were prohibited from buying land or leasing it for a period of more than 31 years. Catholic children were barred from attending foreign schools, and it was made very difficult for them to attend and graduate from Trinity College Dublin, the country's only university.

The most seismic change was the requirement that land owned by a Catholic had to be divided equally among all his sons when he died, unless the eldest son converted to Protestantism; in which case he would inherit the entire estate. Over the years, the larger Catholic landholdings were slowly divided into smaller and smaller pieces. While Parliament didn't go so far as to ban the practice of Catholicism itself, all bishops, monks and friars were sent into exile. Priests were allowed to remain, but had to wear identifying badges at all times. Finally, in 1728, the last of the Penal Laws deprived all Catholics of the right to vote.

At the beginning of the 18th century, Catholics comprised nearly 75 per cent of the Irish population, but all wealth and power were in the hands of Protestants, the 'Ascendancy'. They began to rebuild large parts of Dublin, replacing the dirty claustrophobic alleyways with broad streets and squares. By 1800 Dublin was one of the finest cities in Europe.

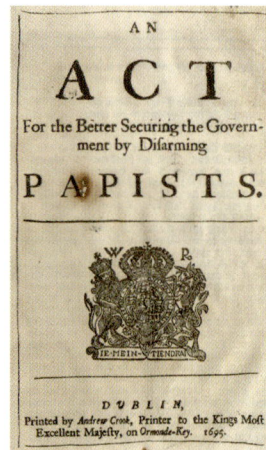

Printed copy of the Penal Laws.

Meanwhile, poor Catholics in the countryside were living in tiny, overcrowded hovels, scratching a living. Some died of starvation, especially in the harsh winters of 1739–41 when widespread crop failure caused famine across Europe. In Ireland almost 400,000 people died of hunger and disease.

A British satire on the efforts of Charles James Fox to get the Test and Corporation Acts repealed. The legislation required membership of the Church of England, as well as other religious and civil obligations, for anyone seeking public office.

Jonathan Swift (1667–1745), satirist, studio of Charles Jervas (c.1675–1739).

With the power to block and enact Irish legislation, the English Parliament could suppress any Irish industry that might have a detrimental effect upon the markets in England. When it banned the export of Irish wool, thus destroying the Irish woollen industry, it caught the attention of the Irish satirist, Jonathan Swift.

Swift was born in Dublin in 1667. His father was English, and he received a good education and later a good living in the Church of Ireland. He had no great love for Ireland and left the country for England as soon as he could. Driven by ambition, he penned government propaganda in the hope of being awarded a bishopric in the Church of England. In 1713, he was appointed dean of St Patrick's Cathedral in Dublin and returned to the country of his birth. There he saw at first-hand the effects of the Penal Laws. Although he was no champion of Ireland, still less of Catholicism, England's gratuitous cruelty and injustice struck a chord.

In 1720, Swift wrote *A Proposal for the Universal Use of Irish Manufacture*, which called upon the people of Ireland to boycott all English products in favour of goods made in Ireland.

He now had the bit between his teeth, and between 1724 and 1735 he wrote a series of seven pamphlets, *The Drapier's Letters*, in which he attacked the various abuses of the English Parliament, arguing that Ireland should be able to enact its own legislation, unhindered. Swift became a hero in Ireland, and not just for his support of the people. When he died in 1745, he bequeathed the enormous sum of £12,000 (more than £3.5/€4.2 million today) to build 'a house for fools and mad'. St Patrick's, one of the first psychiatric hospitals in the world, was founded in Dublin in 1746.

Swift's writings helped to provoke a new sense of Irish nationalism. Perhaps for the first time in the history of Ireland, the people began to unite in the face of a common enemy.

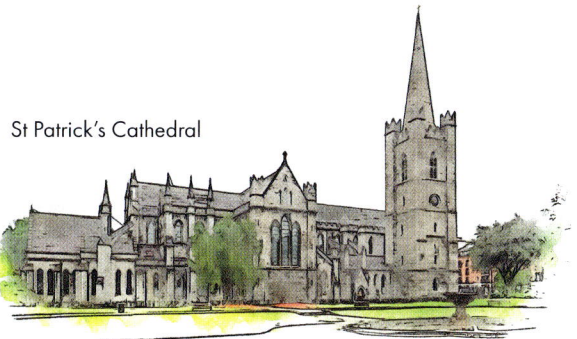

St Patrick's Cathedral

In the winter of 1739/40, disaster struck. In mid-December 1739, after weeks of cold, wet and windy weather, a hard frost set in across Europe.

That winter is still the coldest winter on record. It was so cold that birds fell dead from the trees and the rivers froze over. Even the prawns in Dublin Bay froze to death. The moving parts in the flour mills seized up so no grain could be ground, depriving the people of one of their most important food sources. By the middle of January 1740, starvation was rife. With most pre-industrial manufacturing machinery out of action because of the extreme cold, there was very little employment. The government took no action to help the starving population, who had to rely on the charity of the wealthy, some of whom were very generous. The Duke of Devonshire, Lord Lieutenant of Ireland, donated his own money to famine relief and banned the export of corn. He invited the composer Handel to premiere his new oratorio, *The Messiah*, in Dublin, with some of the proceeds going to famine relief.

At this time, the potato was not the staple food in Ireland – grains were a more important part of the Irish diet. When the extreme cold had abated

there was a two-month drought which killed many of the animals that had survived the freezing temperatures. The grain crops failed and food prices rose sharply. Although the famine continued and worsened throughout 1741, the government still took no action. Dysentery and fever were rife. Some estimates put the death toll at 500,000, out of a population of 2.5 million.

In August 1741 five shiploads of grain from America arrived in Galway, and the harvest that year, while not back to normal, was relatively good. People stopped hoarding and food prices finally returned to normal.

After the famine, people became more dependent on the potato – an ideal crop for growing on small plots of poor land. By 1780 it had become the staple food of the native people of Ireland. This shift would have devastating consequences.

Winter landscape with bird trap,
Pieter Brueghel the Elder (1526/1530–1569).

After the famine of 1739–40, life in Ireland began to change for the better. Some of the oppressive Penal Laws, which had been in force for more than a generation, were gradually relaxed or repealed. The population began to increase – early marriage became the norm among the native Irish and it was cheap to feed children with potatoes. New industries were set up all over the island. Ireland's great forests were stripped away, either for logging or for pastureland, or for heavy industries like iron smelting. The harbours were expanded to accommodate an increase in trade. A new, mainly Catholic, business class appeared – the new businessmen had grown up under the educational restrictions of the Penal Laws and seized the new opportunities that were being made available to them.

The government in England did its best to hamper Ireland's development, imposing high tariffs on the successful Irish linen and glass industries, and sometimes even banning exports outright. When the Irish began to brew beer in quantity (Arthur Guinness founded his brewery in Dublin in 1759), England blocked the export of hops to Ireland, creating and protecting a monopoly for English beers. Jonathan Swift had been lauded for writing about such abuses, and the Irish people were not going to accept them without a fight.

The crunch came in 1751, when the Irish treasury found itself with a surplus. Britain claimed the money in the name of the king, which provoked anger in many quarters. When 1753 brought another surplus, the Irish Parliament, led by Henry Boyle, lobbied hard to retain the money. They succeeded. This enormous victory led to the birth of a new Irish parliamentary group – the Patriots.

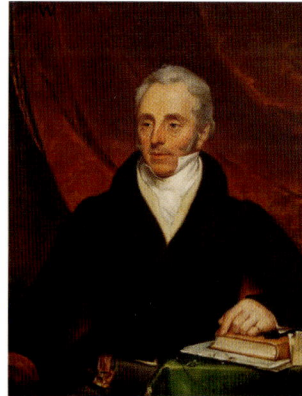

Arthur Guinness, (1768–1855), Martin Gregan.

The Irish House of Commons, 1780,
Francis Wheatley (1747–1801).

The success of the Patriots in the Irish Parliament in the 1750s was short-lived. They were gradually stripped of power by the strong hand of a succession of British viceroys. A new opportunity presented itself in 1775, when the American

Portrait of Henry Grattan 1746–1820, Thomas Alfred Jones (1823–1893), after James Ramsay (1786–1854).

colonies revolted against British rule. The British troops stationed in Ireland were withdrawn or sent to fight in America, and the treasury was emptied to fund the war.

In 1778 the Irish Parliament, now led by Patriot lawyer Henry Grattan, was allowed to raise a Protestant militia force in 1778. By 1779, more than 40,000 Volunteers had signed up. Supported by many Catholics, the Volunteers soon became a force for political change.

Fired by Grattan's stirring oratory, the Irish lobbied Britain for the repeal of its invidious trade legislation. The Patriot leaders knew that Ireland needed full legislative independence. The British Parliament could still enact or overturn any Irish legislation and could reinstate any of the oppressive trade laws at any time.

The Irish Parliament opened in 1782 against the backdrop of a completely different political landscape in Britain. The war in America had been lost and the Tories had been swept from office. With a weakened foe, the time to strike had come.

On 25 February 1782, the leaders of the Volunteers met at Dungannon and produced a

declaration demanding legislative independence for the Irish Parliament. On 16 April 1782, Henry Grattan rose in the Irish Parliament and uttered a strident call for freedom. England, weakened by the American war and unable to face yet another revolution, finally gave way.

This was the dawn of a new era in Irish politics. 'Grattan's Parliament' endured for the next 20 years.

The Dublin Volunteers on College Green, 4th November 1779, Francis Wheatley, (1747–1801).

Peep of Day Boy's Preventing an Union by Adding Fire to the Sun. An Irish Method of Throwing Cold Water on a Subject!

Isaac Cruikshank (1764–1811).

By the second half of the 18th century, Ireland was finally enjoying legislative independence. The economy was booming as new industries provided work and income. The huge increase in the population put pressure on the availability of farming land. People moved to the cities to find work in the new industries and overcrowding led to the creation of slums, especially in Dublin. The situation exacerbated the tension between the different religious groups. Irish Catholics in the north had to compete for land with Presbyterians of Scottish descent, while the English Protestant minority continued to hold most of the land and the political power.

In 1759, Britain removed its restrictions on Irish cattle imports. New legislation closed off large areas of common land for grazing, known as 'enclosures', to the detriment of many Irish Catholics who farmed and lived on the land.

The threatened Irish responded by forming secret bands of night-time marauders who destroyed enclosures, maimed livestock and assaulted the local cattlemen. They were known as 'Whiteboys', because of the white smocks they wore over their clothes.

Presbyterians in Ulster also formed societies and began a campaign of terror against their English landlords. Catholics and Presbyterians had to compete for dwindling land resources, and both turned to the secret societies. The modus operandi of the Presbyterian Peep O' Day Boys was to launch attacks on their enemies at first light. The Catholic Defenders went on the offensive and the violence began to spiral out of control.

On 21 September 1795, the two groups met in a skirmish at a crossroads known as the Diamond, near Loughgall, County Armagh. The Peep O' Day Boys fired shots into an attacking group of Defenders, killing dozens of them. After the Battle of the Diamond, the Peep O' Day Boys renamed their society the Orange Order, in tribute to their hero, King William of Orange. The new order would have an impact on the politics of Northern Ireland for the next two centuries.

*Portrait of Theobald Wolfe Tone (1763–1798),
Unknown Artist, Ireland, 18th century.*

In 1791, a young Dublin-born lawyer, Theobald Wolfe Tone, released a pamphlet entitled *An Argument on Behalf of the Catholics of Ireland*. It was based on the ideals of justice, liberty and the rights of man, recently popularised by Thomas Paine. Tone argued that Catholics and Protestants would both benefit from uniting politically. These radical ideas were picked up by Henry Grattan, and, later that year, a group of Irish Volunteers from Belfast, inspired by the French Revolution and its call for equality, invited Tone to help found a new organisation, to be known as the Society of United Irishmen. The aim of the society was the reform of the Irish Parliament. The founding members were all Protestants, but many Catholics had soon joined the society. It had its own newspaper, the *Northern Star*, which soon boasted the highest readership in the country. However, despite the popularity of the society, most Protestant parliamentarians were unmoved by its aims and ideals.

The following year the oppressed masses in France rose up and the country was plunged into the Reign of Terror. The government in England, contemplating the oppressed masses that made up the majority of the Irish population, became nervous.

The United Irish Patriots of 1798.

In 1793, Henry Grattan and Wolfe Tone travelled to England with the Catholic Committee, set up to campaign for the relief of the civil and political disabilities of Catholics, for a meeting with King George III and Prime Minister William Pitt the Younger. The delegates returned to Ireland with firm assurances of help. Later that year, the Irish Parliament voted to repeal almost all of the remaining Penal Laws. Catholics could now own land and vote in parliamentary elections, but they were still barred from serving in parliament and other top government positions. While Irish Catholics celebrated, the Society of United Irishmen knew that their work was as yet unfinished.

End of the Irish Invasion. — or — The Destruction of the French Armada.

James Gillray (1756–1815), satirical hand-coloured etching of French warships and participants in the rebellion.

In 1795 William, Fourth Earl Fitzwilliam, arrived in Dublin as Lord Lieutenant of Ireland and encouraged Henry Grattan to put forward a bill for the repeal of the last remaining Penal Laws. Despite Fitzwilliam's support, the Emancipation Bill, which proposed full Catholic emancipation, was defeated in Parliament. Many of the United Irishmen now saw no future in peaceful negotiation and began to plot rebellion. When they looked to France for military assistance, Wolfe Tone was arrested for meeting with a French spy and avoided prosecution only by going into voluntary exile in America. While there, he continued to receive funds from the United Irishmen so that he could seek the assistance of the French.

In 1796 Tone left America for France, and persuaded the French government that Ireland stood on the brink of rebellion. The French organised a vast expedition of more than 14,000 soldiers, equipped with a large supply of arms and munitions, to sail to Ireland to fan the fires of revolution, but the attempt at a military invasion had a somewhat farcical conclusion. Forced by the strength of the Royal Navy to sail during the inclement winter season, the expedition departed from Brest on 15 December 1796. The ships became separated during a storm, and although most of the fleet did eventually arrive in Bantry Bay on 22 December, the horrendous weather prevented a landing, and the expedition had to be abandoned. All the ships returned to France, but not before the British realised that they had had an enemy force on their doorstep.

They moved quickly to round up the leaders of the United Irishmen, but it was too late. In May 1798, Ireland exploded into open rebellion.

Léopold Le Guen (1828 – 1895), the battle between French and British warships.

In 1796, the government, alarmed at the continuing violence between the Defenders and the Orange Order in Ulster, passed the Insurrection Act. This gave an enormous amount of power to the local British commander, General Gerard Lake. Lake set up a network of spies and informants and was able to round up most of the leaders of the United Irishmen. He recruited yeomen locally and sent them around the countryside in search of the group's weapons.

Gruesome execution of prisoners by the rebels on the bridge at Wexford in an engraving by George Cruikshank.

The yeomen's methods were brutal and their tactics had soon pushed many thousands to join the United Irishmen and the Defenders. The last United Irishman leader still at large, Lord Edward FitzGerald, declared that they would rise up on 23 May 1798. Although he was arrested on 19 May, the rising went ahead without him. Within two days, thousands had taken up mostly makeshift arms, mainly pikes and farm implements, and had fought over a dozen battles in County Kildare. In most places, they were easily defeated by the British forces. The bloody reprisals of the British brought out the people of Counties Wicklow and Wexford, who rose up in a rebellion under the leadership of a Catholic priest, Father John Murphy. The rebels gained control of the city of Wexford and declared the Irish Republic. However, the United Irishmen and Defenders lacked central leadership and were ultimately no match for the well-trained and highly organised British military.

The British forces drove the rebels back until they reached Vinegar Hill, just outside Wexford. Almost 20,000 Irish rebels, armed with pikes, faced 10,000 well-armed British troops backed by cannons. The British soon had the rebels on the run. They drove them through the streets of Wexford, in a rampage of merciless slaughter.

Lake's bloody enthusiasm in putting down the rising may have alarmed the government. He was recalled to Britain and was replaced by Lord Cornwallis, who had a reputation for tolerance. He quickly granted an amnesty, bringing the rebellion to an end.

General Lake

At the time of the 1798 rebellion, the population of Ireland was almost half that of Great Britain, and events had made the government keenly aware of the dangers of instability. Prime Minister William Pitt appointed Robert Stewart, Lord Castlereagh, as Chief Secretary, instructing him to work with Lord Cornwallis on an Act of Union that would merge the parliaments of Britain and Ireland.

Many in Ireland were open to the idea of any change that might reduce the threat of more violence. Cornwallis and Castlereagh made their first approaches to Catholic Church leaders, indicating that the Act of Union would lead to full Catholic emancipation. Most Irish Catholics came out in support of union, but the majority of the Irish parliamentarians did not.

When Parliament reconvened in January 1799, the Act of Union passed by only a single vote; the slim margin meant that the legislation was never promulgated.

On 15 January 1800, Castlereagh again brought the legislation before Parliament. Henry Grattan, who had come out of retirement for the purpose, led the opposition to the Act of Union, but this time it was passed by a comfortable majority of 60 votes.

A year later, the Irish Parliament was dissolved and 100 Irish MPs took up their seats in the House of Commons in Westminster, together with 32

Portrait of the Right Honourable William Pitt the Younger (1759–1806), John Hoppner (1758–1810), detail.

new members of the House of Lords. For the time being the two countries kept their own treasuries, but together they formed one nation – the United Kingdom of Great Britain and Ireland.

William Pitt now focused on Catholic emancipation, but despite the hints and promises of Castlereagh and Cornwallis, it soon became clear that neither king nor parliament would countenance it. In the face of such opposition, Pitt resigned, as did Lords Cornwallis and Castlereagh.

Charles, Second Earl and First Marquess Cornwallis (1738–1805), Thomas Gainsborough (1727–1788).

Robert Stewart, Second Marquess of Londonderry (Lord Castlereagh), Thomas Lawrence (1769–1830) detail.

Life in Ireland in the immediate aftermath of the Act of Union went on much as before. The Protestants were still at the top of the pile, and there were sporadic outbursts of violence. To maintain control, the government had almost 25,000 British soldiers permanently stationed in Ireland.

The United Irishmen found a new leader in Robert Emmet. He had inherited money and used it to set up clandestine weapons factories around the city of Dublin. He also invented new types of explosive, including rockets and grenades. He met with other revolutionary groups in and around the city and formulated a plan to seize Dublin Castle, the heart of the British administration in Ireland.

On 23 May 1803 he instructed his men to gather at a local tavern, while he found coaches to take them to Dublin Castle. Only about 80 of his recruits showed up at the rendezvous, and those that did started drinking. Then Emmet learned that

Lord Kilwarden and his son were pulled from their coach and assassinated by a drunken mob.

Execution of Robert Emmet in Thomas Street, Dublin.

the weapons he had manufactured were useless, because of some confusion surrounding the fuses. When the coaches arrived, the coach drivers realised that something was not quite right and drove off. Instead of calling the whole thing off, Emmet drew his sword and led his drunken band of men to Dublin Castle on foot. They were armed only with pikes, and had soon melted away. At that point, Emmet gave up and went home.

Unfortunately, Emmet's drunken mob didn't just slink home, but rampaged through the streets of Dublin. When they happened across the chief justice, Lord Kilwarden, they pulled him from his coach and stabbed both him and his son to death.

A month after the failed rebellion, the authorities tracked Emmet down and arrested him. He was tried for high treason, condemned to death and hanged on 20 September 1803. Despite the abject failure of his attempted rebellion, Emmet's rousing speech from the dock ensured him a permanent place in Ireland's pantheon of heroes.

In 1804, Henry Grattan, despite his opposition to the Act of Union, campaigned for a seat in the Westminster parliament and refocused his energies on Catholic emancipation. The Catholic Relief Act of 1793 had given the vote to anyone in Ireland who owned the minimum 40 shillings' worth of property, the '40-shilling freeholders', but Catholics still had no representation in Parliament. Grattan gathered support for his movement, and saw the margin of defeat for his emancipation bills shrink each time they were put to the vote. In 1819, his bill lost by a mere two votes, then Grattan died in 1820 before he could present it again. Although his supporters put forward a new bill later that year that passed the House of Commons, it was rejected by the House of Lords.

Most of the Irish felt completely betrayed. They needed another hero to spearhead the campaign for emancipation and found one in Daniel O'Connell. A Catholic lawyer educated in France and England, O'Connell had returned to Ireland in 1797, just as rebellion was spreading across the country. Witnessing the horror and bloodshed, O'Connell decided to campaign for change through peaceful means. Over the next quarter of a century, he built his reputation as a lawyer, while working to unite his Catholic countrymen. In 1823 he founded a new political organisation, the Catholic Association, and, in 1824, he decided to reduce the membership fee to an affordable penny a month. Membership of the association exploded. The Catholic Church helped to collect the membership fees, known as 'Catholic Rent'. In its first year the Catholic Association managed to raise the huge sum of £20,000. The British government believed that the existence of the association would lead to civil war in Ireland and outlawed it in 1825. To get around this, O'Connell founded 'The New Catholic Association' four months later, and listed amongst its principles full compliance with the laws of Britain.

Daniel O'Connell: The Champion of Liberty, poster published in Pennsylvania, 1847.

In 1825 Catholic emancipation seemed as distant as ever. Stymied by the impossibility of being elected to parliament, some Catholics in Waterford decided to nominate a Protestant to run against the local landlord in the 1826 parliamentary election as an 'emancipation' candidate. Previous legislation had extended the franchise to all 40-shilling freeholders, but the ballot was open, so voting against a landlord's wishes was risky. However, when O'Connell later lent the support of the Catholic Association, offering to support any Catholics who fell foul of their landlord by failing to vote for his chosen candidate, the emancipation candidate won by a landslide.

Two years later, and with two emancipation candidates in Parliament, O'Connell discovered a legal loophole. The remaining Penal Laws didn't actually bar a Catholic from being elected to Parliament; but taking up a seat at Westminster required the taking of an oath that no Catholic could ever take. So, when a by-election was forced in County Clare in 1828, O'Connell stood for election. More than 30,000 Catholic Association supporters descended on a town that had just 3,000 voters. O'Connell won the seat, and when he arrived at Parliament, he refused to take the oath.

The British government capitulated on the subject of Catholic emancipation and, in 1829, the Catholic Emancipation Act became law. O'Connell, now given the title 'Liberator of the Nation', took his seat in Parliament, while the Catholic Association disbanded.

However, the British government had the last word. The minimum freeholding for Irish voters was raised from 40 shillings to £10. Overnight, the 40-shilling freeholders, more than 90 per cent of the Irish electorate, who had been given the vote in 1793, were disenfranchised.

Opposite: Punch, 26 August, 1843. Irish peasants pay homage to their 'kin' on the Hill of Tara. O'Connell enthroned upon the devil, with his foot on the British Constitution.

Above: Catholic Petitioners or Symptoms of a Peaceable Appeal. A cartoon depicting Daniel O'Connell leading an angry mob towards London, trampling upon the Oath of Allegiance and holding the Catholic rent roll, the source of funds for the Catholic Association.

Having achieved Catholic emancipation, Daniel O'Connell decided to push for repeal of the Act of Union. There was little will for change at Westminster, and public opinion in Ireland was split. The north of Ireland had prospered since 1801 – the sectarian violence that had troubled the region had decreased with the uptick in employment that came with the boom in industry. The south, however, with a much higher Catholic population and largely dependent on agriculture, saw little benefit from the Union.

In 1838, O'Connell decided to fight for repeal in much the same way as he had campaigned for emancipation. His initial attempts at gaining support in the north triggered unrest, so he turned to the south and its more receptive population. He set up the Repeal Association, modelled on the very successful Catholic Association. The membership fee was the same, one penny a month, referred to as 'Repeal Rent'. The money was soon flowing in.

Young Ireland, which had been founded in 1842 by Thomas Davis, Charles Gavan Duffy and John Blake Dillon to campaign for independence, supported O'Connell in his drive for repeal, as did the Catholic Church.

O'Connell continued to espouse a non-violent approach to political change. His tactic with the Repeal Association was to hold 'Monster Meetings' around the country. He was a renowned orator and people flocked to the meetings from miles around to hear him speak. He hoped that the enormous attendances would intimidate the Westminster government. They did. A 'Monster Meeting' was planned for 8 October 1843 at Clontarf, near Dublin, site of Brian Boru's great victory over the Vikings. On 7 October, the government banned the gathering and O'Connell called it off. He was arrested and convicted of a spurious charge of conspiracy and was sentenced to a year in prison. His conviction was overturned three months later.

Sir Charles Gavan Duffy

O'Connell now compromised on repeal, calling for a separate Irish Parliament to decide on domestic issues, with Westminster controlling foreign affairs. This lost him some popular support and created a rift with Young Ireland.

Daniel O'Connell, M.P., (1775–1847), addressing his supporters at 'The Monster Meeting of the 20th September 1843 at Clifden', County Galway, Joseph Patrick Haverty (1794–1864).

There was nothing unusual about the weather on Saturday, 6 January 1839 – it was dull and cold, with some snow showers. There was a light breeze in the afternoon and it was reported to have become quite warm. By 9 o'clock that evening, however, things were beginning to take a very unexpected turn. Dublin was experiencing a westerly gale, which had become a 'strong gale' by midnight and had then turned into a hurricane-force wind. In some areas there were reports of a tornado, or 'whirlwind'. The wind didn't subside until the small hours of Sunday morning. The whole country experienced similar phenomena, and daybreak revealed scenes of utter devastation. A week later, the *Dublin Evening Post* described it as 'the most awful calamity with which a people were afflicted'.

It is estimated that 200 people died as a result of the storm that night. Dublin was described as having the appearance of a 'sacked city'. Countless head of livestock had lost their lives. Harvest stores were destroyed. People woke up to find their roofs gone; some buildings were partially demolished. Thatched houses, particularly, were ignited by embers from the domestic hearth, and several people lost their lives in house fires. Trees were uprooted and carried away by the force of the wind. Salty brine was found on trees 40 miles inland, and fish were scattered over fields, having been lifted out of the sea by the force of the wind. The canal near Kilbeggan in County Westmeath was reported to have been completely emptied of water by the wind.

The devastation was unprecedented, but it could have been much worse. Everyone had a horror story to tell, but many people had had lucky escapes and there was an outpouring of neighbourliness in the wake of the storm. As it turned out, the calamity of the Big Wind was just a precursor to the catatastrophe of the Great Famine, which began a mere six years later.

Vessels in a Storm at the Mouth of a Harbour, 1858, Thomas Frederick Collier (1831–1891.

Perhaps the single most important event in modern Irish history, the potato famine led to the deaths of nearly a million people and the emigration of over a million more.

Having seen the Irish population grow from five million in 1800 to over eight million in 1841, many in government worried that the small island could no longer fully support its inhabitants. In 1844, the government-appointed Devon Commission noted that huge segments of the population lived in abject poverty. By 1845, as many as three million Irish were wholly dependent on the potato for food. Blight was first noticed on potatoes in September 1845, and by mid-November it was apparent that the crop had failed. Then, in 1846, a new blight struck Ireland, mainly in Ulster and along the west coast.

Prime Minister Robert Peel responded quickly. Quietly spending £1 million on American corn, Peel sent the food to Ireland and distributed it to the hungry. For a while it appeared that the crisis might be averted, but then two events changed the history of Ireland. In late 1846, Peel was driven from power, and in 1847 the potato blight returned. The blight of 1847 devastated the entire island. The government instituted a work-for-food programme. It was an unwieldy, bureaucratic nightmare. Hunger killed the Irish in their thousands, and with starvation came its usual companions, sickness and disease. Despite the dreadful situation of the people, grain continued to be exported from Ireland to Britain. The government refused to stop the exports, fearing that to do so might upset the market.

Others tried desperately to fight the crisis. The Quakers set up food kitchens. American sympathisers and others sent food and money to Ireland. However, the numbers of dead climbed into the hundreds of thousands, and the increasing desperation started a mass migration.

The year 1849 brought another ruined crop, followed by a massive outbreak of cholera. The blight failed to return in 1850, but by that time a quarter of the population had been wiped away; a million dead, a million more fled.

Burying the child. Painting by Lillian Lucy Davidson (1879–1954).

People had been leaving Ireland in search of a better life since the mid-18th century, but from 1845 emigration escalated to previously unimagined levels. The famine relief schemes started by the government in 1846–7 were stopped at the end of 1847, long before the potato blight and the suffering were over. In desperation, people began to emigrate, sometimes paying their own fares but often at the expense of landowners happy to get them off their land. Between 1845 and 1855, over a million Irish left their homeland, most for the New World. Thousands died of cholera during the ocean crossing, crammed aboard overloaded ships that became known as 'coffin ships'. More died while trying to clear customs, or attempting to walk from Canada to the US. Even so, hundreds of thousands made it through the horrors to establish new homes on foreign shores, creating Irish enclaves that would play an important part in the future of Ireland.

Emigration and famine memory evoked strong nationalist feelings in the Irish communities that formed in cities across the globe, especially in the US. Most of those fleeing the famine arrived penniless and were unable to move on from the cities where they landed, leading to large Irish populations in the US cities of the eastern seaboard – by 1860, in the cities of Boston, Baltimore, New York and Philadelphia, 25 per cent of the population was Irish. Although St Patrick's Day had been celebrated in some parts of America since the first half of the 18th century, it was after the major famine emigration that it became a regular occurrence. The rousing keynote speeches delivered at the annual St Patrick's Day parades were soon focusing on the oppression of the Irish people by the British and calling for donations towards the heroic struggle this necessitated.

On board an emigrant ship, tending to the sick.

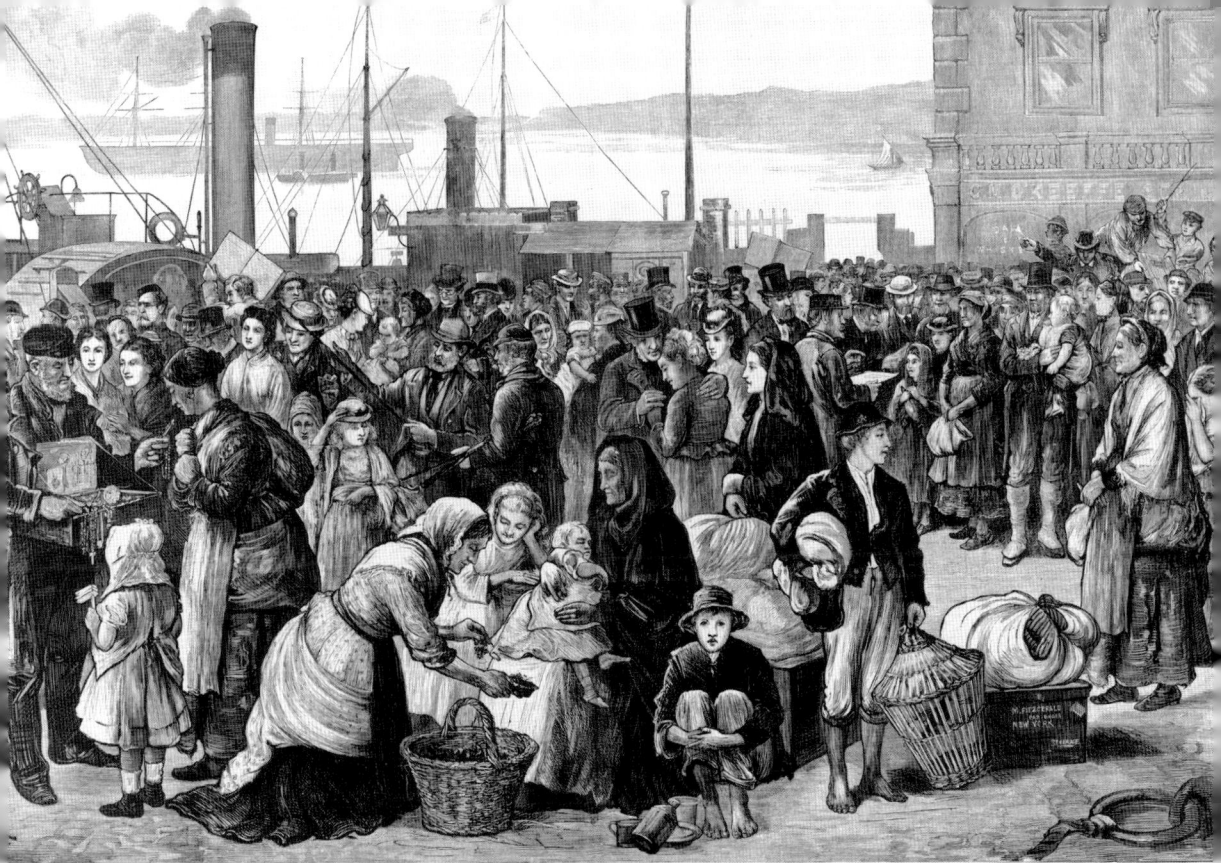

Emigrants leaving Queenstown, now known as Cobh, for New York, 1874. Cobh was the major Irish port of emigrant embarkation for North America.

In 1858, Young Irelander James Stephens founded the Irish Republican Brotherhood (IRB). It aimed to rid Ireland of the British, clearing the path for the foundation of an Irish Republic. He was supported by Irish expatriates in the US, including John O'Mahony, who had founded the Fenian Brotherhood, or Fenians. While they were recruiting for the cause, the American Civil War broke out in 1861, providing an opportunity for Fenians and other Irish volunteers to gain useful military experience. The war ended in 1865, with thousands of veteran expatriate and native Irish soldiers eager to fight for the cause of Irish freedom. Stephens hesitated – and was lost. Britain had been infiltrating the IRB for several years, and many of the IRB leaders, including Stephens himself, were arrested.

The IRB rescued Stephens from jail, but the organisation had lost its focus. In May 1866, a group of Fenians launched an attack from New York into Canada, defeating a Canadian brigade at the Battle of Lime Ridge, but were later defeated by a force from the US. The IRB launched a revolution in March 1867. Thousands marched on centres of British authority in Ireland, but they had

Colourised photograph of James Stephens (1824–1901), Irish Republican and the founding member of the Fenian movement in Dublin in 1858, later to become known as the Irish Republican Brotherhood, or IRB.

no proper leadership and the rebellion was easily put down by the Irish constabulary, in most cases without violence.

Although the IRB and Fenian uprisings were unsuccessful in the military sense, they did succeed in disturbing British complacency about the plight of the people of Ireland. The IRB continued to grow in importance, going on to play a role as Ireland's largest secret revolutionary organisation, up to the Easter Rising of 1916, but their most important legacy was the awakening of the British consciousness to Ireland's situation.

John Francis O'Mahony, Irish Republican and Colonel to the 69th Regiment of New York State Militia in the Union Army, c.1865.

In 1823 a newspaper called the *Irish Times* was founded, but it was short-lived and closed down in 1825. In 1859, Major Lawrence Knox, a 22-year-old Protestant army officer, adopted the name for his new newspaper. Following his own politics, it was intended to be the voice of Protestant nationalism.

The first edition of Knox's *Irish Times* was published on 29 March 1859, as a 'new conservative daily paper'. At first, however, it was published only on Tuesdays, Thursdays and Saturdays. After an initial period of 14 weeks, from 8 June 1859 it was published daily from offices at 4 Lower Abbey Street, Dublin, joining the ranks of nine other Irish newspapers. Its main competitor at that time was the Dublin *Daily Express,* a unionist newspaper.

Knox died in 1873 and the newspaper was bought by the Arnott family (of the Arnotts department stores) of Dublin. The politics of the paper shifted, and it became the mouthpiece of southern unionism. The newspaper moved to offices on D'Olier Street in 1895, and was soon nicknamed 'the Old Lady of D'Olier Street'. In 1900 it became a public company, and in 1916 it

The founder of the *Irish Times*: Major Lawrence Edward Knox (1836–1873).

added its voice to those calling for the execution of the leaders of the Easter Rising. It shifted to an independent political line after the establishment of the Irish Free State in 1922.

The editor during the 1930s, R.M. Smyllie, opposed Franco during the Spanish Civil War, angering the Irish Catholic hierarchy. During the Second World War, battling with censorship, the *Irish Times* supported the Allies, in opposition to the de Valera government's policy of neutrality.

In 1974 a trust was formed to maintain the *Irish Times* as 'an independent newspaper primarily concerned with serious issues for the benefit of the community throughout the whole of Ireland, free from any form of personal or party political, commercial, religious or other sectional control'.

The first editon of the *Irish Times*.

William Butler Yeats, poet, playwright, senator and Nobel laureate, Ireland's most famous literary son, was born in 1865, at the height of the Victorian era. His family belonged to the Anglo-Irish Protestant ascendancy, which was then on the brink of losing its privileged position in Ireland. His education was patchy and the fact that he achieved international recognition as a genius is largely due to his habit of reading widely and his enquiring mind. This self-made man would become a towering literary presence.

Lady Gregory, portrait by William Orpen, c.1904.

Yeats loved the country of his birth and always made much of his Irishness. When Ireland was about to gain independence from Britain, he committed himself politically and culturally to the emerging state. He was one of the founders of the Irish Literary Revival and was key to its success in reintroducing the population to its folkloric heritage. With Lady Gregory, he founded the national theatre (now the Abbey Theatre) and was one of its directors. His youthful membership of the Young Ireland Society and the Irish Republican Brotherhood led to his being appointed a senator in the first Free State government in 1922.

In 1923 Yeats was awarded the Nobel Prize for Literature, the first of 13 Irish Nobel laureates in the fields of science, literature, peacemaking and the promotion of human rights.

When Yeats died in 1939 he had achieved international renown and was well on his way to becoming Ireland's favourite poet. His legacy, though, extends further than his poetry – he was instrumental in bringing Irish culture and language back to life for the emerging nation.

W.B. Yeats, painted by his
father, John Butler Yeats.

When people began to emigrate from Ireland in large numbers in order to flee the Great Famine, an estimated one million people flooded Liverpool between January and April 1847. Many of those did not have the passage money for the onward journey to the New World and opted to stay in England. By 1861, more than 15 per cent of the Manchester population was Irish. Fenianism found fertile political ground here, offering solidarity and liberation to the exploited working Irish.

On 11 September 1867, two high-profile Fenians from the US, Thomas J. Kelly and Timothy Deasy, were arrested in Manchester. Their police convoy was attacked by about 40 Fenian sympathisers en route to Belle Vue Prison and a police officer was killed, by accident rather than design.

There was outrage from the anti-nationalist British establishment, who were soon baying for blood. On 8 October, reflecting popular opinion, *The Times* called for 'a stern and decisive repression'. The police embarked on indiscriminate raids of the Irish areas of Manchester, arresting 29 people. After a suspiciously quick and procedurally dubious

trial, five men, Thomas Maguire, Edward Condon, William Allen, Michael Larkin and Michael O'Brien, were found guilty of the murder of the police officer and were sentenced to be hanged. None of them had fired the fatal shot. Maguire was reprieved and Condon (a US citizen) had his sentence commuted after the intervention of the US government, but Allen, Larkin and O'Brien were hanged on 23 November 1867 before a crowd of 8,000–10,000 outside the New Bailey Prison in Salford. They were soon being mythologised by the Fenian propaganda machine as the 'Manchester Martyrs'.

The New Bailey Prison, Salford.

Allen, Larkin and O'Brien, executed at Manchester
in 1867.

William Ewart Gladstone became prime minister of Britain in December 1868. He brought fresh and sympathetic eyes to the Irish question and saw that injustice was rife in the country.

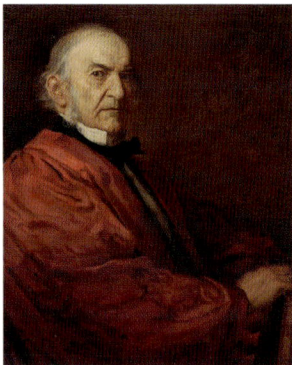

Portrait of William Ewart Gladstone (1809–1898) C.H. Thompson (1870–1946).

Out of a population of over six million, only around 700,000 Irish people belonged to the so-called 'national' church, the Protestant Church of Ireland, to which everyone, Catholic and Protestant, had to pay a tithe. Gladstone introduced legislation that brought an end to the national church in Ireland. Although the church was allowed to keep the buildings it used for worship, the rest of the land was transferred to the government.

The government offered favourable loans for the purchase of the land, and thousands of Irish were able to buy property for the first time. Gladstone then looked at the ongoing land disputes that had arisen because unscrupulous landlords had been milking their Irish tenants for every penny. In 1870, he put forward a bill to protect tenants from being evicted unfairly. The House of Lords completely reworked it, ripping the teeth out of the legislation before sending it back to the

An Irish landlord begging for rent, 19th-century cartoon.

Commons. The inadequacy of the resulting Land Act of 1870 outraged the people of Ireland and unleashed the period of violence and lawlessness that became known as the Land War.

Gladstone's party, the Liberals, lost the 1874 general election and the next administration completely ignored Ireland. In 1880, the Liberals won a majority again, and Gladstone returned as prime minister. His Land Act of 1881 gave more protection to Irish tenants, but despite this, the Land War didn't come to an end. To deal with the unrest, Gladstone reluctantly passed stringent anti-coercion legislation, giving the authorities wide powers of arrest and detention. Although this helped to bring an end to the Land War, discontent continued to grow.

Gladstone resigned in 1885, although he would have two more terms as prime minster. They would be notable for his relationship with Charles Stewart Parnell and the great battle for Home Rule.

Evicted, Lady Elizabeth Butler (1846–1933).

After the failure of the Fenian cause in the 1860s, the Irish once again turned to politics to try to right the wrongs of the past. For almost 25 years the campaign for the repeal of the Union had been moribund. Like Daniel O'Connell, the Home Rulers wanted to return to the days of Grattan's Parliament, when Ireland and Britain stood independently under the same monarch. In 1870, former Trinity College professor, Conservative MP and barrister Isaac Butt founded the Irish Home Government Association, to demand 'full control over our domestic affairs'. He had come to the attention of Irish nationalists by his brilliant legal defence of Young Ireland and Fenian prisoners. In 1873 he turned the Home Government Association into a proper political party, the Home Rule Party. In 1874 he was elected to Parliament as its leader.

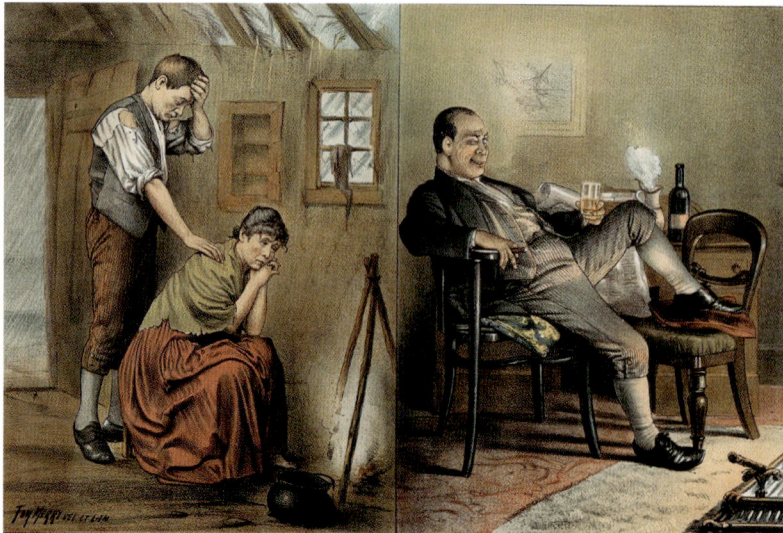

Anti-Home Rule cartoon, 1891. It claims that Home Rule will bring economic benefits to middle-class 'patriots', but ruin to the peasantry.

The same election gave a majority to the Tory party, and Gladstone was out of office for the duration of the new government. The new prime minister, Benjamin Disraeli, was more interested in promoting the British Empire than in solving Ireland's problems, and Butt's attempts to get Ireland back on the agenda came to nothing.

However, the Home Rulers soon found a new champion in Charles Stewart Parnell, a young Protestant landlord from County Wicklow, elected to Westminster for the first time in the 1874 election that had ousted Gladstone and his Liberal government from power.

Isaac Butt, from *Vanity Fair*, May 1873.

Charles Stewart Parnell, an Irish Protestant educated in England, rose quickly through the ranks of the Home Rule Party. In the late 1870s, several years of bad weather in succession destroyed most of the crops in Ireland and plunged thousands of Irish farmers into a debt spiral. Fearful of losing their homes, they formed the Land League, with Parnell as their president. Parnell had secured the support of the IRB, but he insisted that the problem could be solved without resorting to violence. His policy included shunning landlords who unjustly evicted their tenants, or any Irish who took up the tenancy of newly available land. Captain Charles Boycott, the harsh land agent for Lord Erne in Galway, unwittingly gave his name to the practice, and 'boycotting' entered the English language. The disruption that the movement caused became known as the Land War.

In 1881, Gladstone tried to end the Land War by passing a new Land Act, but it was so watered down by the time it was enacted that it was unacceptable to the Land League. Tensions grew and Parnell was arrested. He instantly achieved heroic status and could have launched a rebellion, but he was committed to finding a peaceful solution. Six months after his arrest, Parnell and Gladstone signed the Kilmainham Treaty and Parnell was released from prison. He then threw his support behind the new Land Act.

He now refocused his attention on the question of Home Rule. In the 1885 general election his party secured 85 seats and the Conservatives were ousted. Gladstone and Parnell campaigned for Irish Home Rule, but the issue proved too overwhelming. Gladstone's Liberal Party began to come apart at the seams over the issue, while Parnell's private life mired him in a scandal from which his reputation never recovered.

When the vote for Home Rule came, many Liberals voted against their leader. Home Rule was defeated. Two years later, Parnell, the Blackbird of Avondale, died, aged 45.

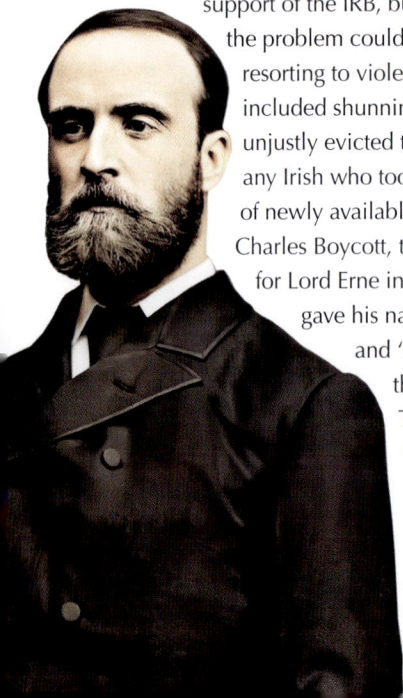

Charles Stewart Parnell

There were many protests over rents. This contemporary engraving
shows unrest at the National Rent Office at Loughrea.

Born in Dublin in 1879 to an English father and an Irish mother, Pádraig Pearse grew up with a rare perspective on the cause of Irish liberty. At the age of 11, he took up the study of the Irish language: its words and its ideals would drive him throughout his life. He studied law at university, but after graduation decided to devote himself to the linked causes of Irish nationalism and education. He wrote poetry in English and Irish, often discussing the plight of Ireland. In 1903 he became the editor of *An Claidheamh Soluis* ('The Sword of Light'), the journal of the Gaelic League, and often lectured in Irish at Trinity College. In 1908, he helped to found St Enda's, a boarding school for young men which infused the curriculum with the nobility of Irish culture.

A long-time supporter of Home Rule, Pearse

Pádraig Pearse

Previously unpublished photo of Pearse as a young boy.

believed that Ireland could never truly be free without a revolution. In 1913, he helped to found the Irish Volunteers, and soon afterwards he joined the IRB, helping to control the Volunteers from the inside. When the First World War caused a fracture in the Volunteers, Pearse used his gifts as orator and writer to shift their ideology from a defence of Home Rule to a revolutionary force.

When the revolution finally came in Easter week of 1916, Pearse marched at the head of the column of troops that seized the General Post Office in Dublin. He then stood on the steps of the post office and read aloud the Proclamation of the Irish Republic that he had signed and helped to draft. For five days, he led his revolutionaries with the power of his words. Then, with Dublin burning around him, he negotiated a surrender in order to prevent more damage to the civilian population.

For the leaders of the Easter Rising, surrender meant certain execution, and Pearse knew it. He faced the firing squad on 3 May 1916.

British soldiers putting prisoners into a truck in a Dublin street, 1916.

On the evening of 6 May 1882, Lord Frederick Cavendish, the Chief Secretary for Ireland, and Thomas Burke, the Permanent Under-Secretary, were ambushed and brutally murdered by seven members of the Irish National Invincibles in the Phoenix Park, Dublin, as they walked towards the Viceregal Lodge. It was Cavendish's first day in the job and it is believed that Burke was the real target – Cavendish was in the wrong place at the wrong time and was killed because he had come to Burke's defence. The original target was W.E. Forster, Cavendish's predecessor, and the Invincibles had failed in several attempts to kill him. His resignation shifted the assassins' focus to Burke. It is unlikely that they were even aware of Cavendish's identity.

The Irish National Invincibles were an extremist splinter group of the IRB with a far more radical agenda. They were formed in 1881 with the specific aim of targeting anyone responsible for the implementation of English policies in Ireland. Chief Secretary Forster, who, from 1879 onwards, had been enthusiastic in his implementation of coercion legislation in response to the Land War, was firmly in their sights. Under-Secretary Burke, Ireland's most senior civil servant, was viewed as his willing accomplice.

The murders were greeted with outrage. Cavendish, who was married to Gladstone's niece, was regarded as sympathetic to the Land League cause and his appointment had been welcomed in Ireland. Five men were convicted of the murders and were executed. Several others received long prison sentences as accessories to the crime.

Parnell condemned the murders unequivocally, but his parliamentary party's alliance with the Liberals to promote the cause of Home Rule disintegrated, ultimately delaying Home Rule by more than a quarter of a century.

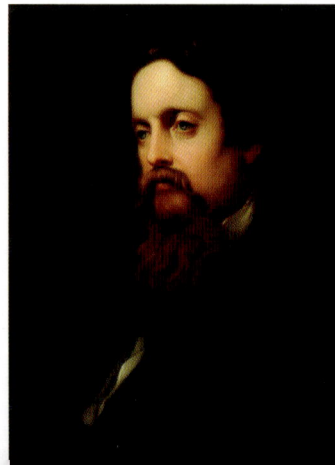

Lord Frederick Cavendish, John D. Miller.

The Phoenix Park Murders of Lord Frederick Cavendish and Thomas Burke, 6 May 1882.

For almost 500 years, the English had suppressed and degraded Irish culture, hampering the people's education and obscuring their rich cultural past. Famine and revolution also took their toll, and by 1851, just under 25 per cent of the population spoke Irish. By the end of the 19th century, that number had dropped below 15 per cent. With a new nationalism sweeping through Ireland, the people began to look to their past to help define what their country would be. They fought to revive what remained of their culture. One of the unique aspects of Ireland's past was sport.

In 1884 Michael Cusack founded the Gaelic Athletic Association (GAA). Cusack had grown up with the English games of rugby and cricket, but he abhorred the social exclusiveness of both sports, which were inaccessible to the lower classes. He created the GAA to promote sport among the Irish of all classes. While the original focus of the GAA was on athletics, the ancient Gaelic games of football and hurling soon came to the fore.

The GAA was a great success. Spectator sports had become very popular in the Victorian era, and in Ireland, partly inspired by the GAA, support for sport became intertwined with the nationalism that was spreading through the country. Within just a few years, the IRB had taken over the GAA, got rid of Cusack and had turned the organisation into one that was increasingly nationalistic. The exclusiveness that Cusack had abhorred now returned, with a ban on GAA members' participation in or attendance at any 'foreign' sporting events. By the early 1900s, the most important GAA matches were attracting over 20,000 spectators. Today, the GAA has over 2,500 clubs in Ireland and interest in Gaelic football and hurling is as strong as ever. It has now dropped most of its nationalist rules, including the ban on watching and playing foreign games. The Irish national rugby team played its home fixtures at the GAA stadium at Croke Park in Dublin from 2007 to 2009, while the rugby stadium at Lansdowne road was being redeveloped.

Colourised photograph of Michael Cusack.

Dr Douglas Hyde (1860–1949), poet, scholar and first President of Ireland, Sarah Henrietta Purser, (1848–1943).

What the GAA had done for the ancient Irish games, others were doing to bring the Irish language back from the brink. In 1893, the Gaelic League, Conradh na Gaeilge, was founded by a group of academics, including Douglas Hyde and Eoin MacNeill, to support the Irish language. The Gaelic League ran classes in Irish and held Irish-speaking social gatherings. Irish had always been a spoken rather than a written language and the League aimed to remedy that for the modern age of literature, funding the publication of new Irish-language poetry and prose. Soon it began to oppose any legislation that it believed would have a detrimental effect on the language, proposing legislation that would actually aid its revival.

The League was intended to be non-political and non-sectarian, and open to everyone interested in keeping Irish language and culture alive. Douglas Hyde believed that the Irish language 'is neither Protestant nor Catholic, it is neither a Unionist nor a Separatist'. However, a large proportion of League members were nationalists. Many of the participants in the 1916 Rising, including signatories of the Proclamation, first met at the League's meetings. Pádraig

Pearse edited the organisation's newspaper, *An Claidheamh Soluis* (The Sword of Light).

Although the Gaelic League and the GAA became involved in nationalistic violence, they managed to survive and prosper. When Ireland achieved independence, the state took on the role of promoting Irish language and culture – Irish was taught in schools, and Gaelic games were played by many from childhood, but English remains the main spoken language in the country. Under a new constitution adopted in 2008, the Gaelic League has a mission to reinstate Irish as the common language of Ireland. With over 200 branches around the country it continues to hold classes, support literature and argue for legislation in support of the language.

An Claidheamh Soluis

In the early years of the 20th century, the Conservatives in Westminster adopted a policy called 'Constructive Unionism', which was designed to kill the idea of Home Rule by kindness.

George Wyndham was appointed Chief Secretary of Ireland in 1900. He worked towards the elimination of the ongoing land issues. In 1902, a landowner named Captain John Shawe-Taylor invited landlords and tenants, both unionist and nationalist, to a conference. The conference recommended a massive government land purchase. Wyndham took up the suggestion, and the 1903 Land Purchase Act became law. The government bought huge tracts of land, then sold small pieces at low-priced, fixed mortgages. Within a decade, Ireland's long-standing land issue had as good as disappeared.

By the time of the Land Act, the Irish Unionists in Parliament had reorganised themselves under John Redmond. In 1910, a close election gave Redmond's Irish Parliamentary Party the deciding votes for government. The Irish returned the Liberals to power under Asquith.

John Redmond (1856–1918), parliamentarian, Harry Jones Thaddeus, (1860–1929).

For years, the House of Lords had been vetoing laws that many perceived to be in the best interests of the country. Supported by the Irish Parliamentary Party, Asquith forced through a constitutional reform. The Lords could still veto legislation, but only for two years in a row. If the House presented a bill for a third consecutive year, the Lords were forced to accept it.

Asquith now put forward a new Home Rule bill, with the intention of creating an independent Irish Parliament to legislate domestic issues, with foreign issues still to be decided at Westminster. The bill passed through the Commons, but was, predictably, vetoed by the Lords. In September 1912, organised by the leader of the Ulster Unionists, Sir Edward Carson, almost 500,000 Ulster men and women signed a covenant opposing Home Rule. The following year, the Unionists formed a militia, the Ulster Volunteer Force.

The First World War erupted in Europe, putting Ireland's problems on hold. The third Home Rule bill became law on 18 September 1914 as the Government of Ireland Act, and was immediately suspended for the duration of the war.

Public auction poster.

When Sinn Féin was founded in 1905 by Arthur Griffith and Bulmer Hobson, it provided a home for some smaller political groups – Fenians, nationalists, pacifists and feminists. Its mission was the establishment of an independent Irish republic and its method was passive resistance. It wanted Irish MPs to withdraw from Westminster and set up a ruling council in Ireland instead, and Irish equivalents of British institutions, such as courts, to be established. Little progress was made in the first 10 years of Sinn Féin's existence, but the outbreak of the First World War altered the situation.

In 1914, when the British army was recruiting in Ireland, Sinn Féin organised demonstrations by pacifists and anti-war activists. The press began to conflate Sinn Féin with the IRB, and in the aftermath of the Easter Rising, when the leaders were executed, there was a huge surge of membership into Sinn Féin, which was believed to have been responsible for the Rising. Overtaken by a new radical element, Sinn Féin called a party convention in October of 1917. Arthur Griffith stood down as president in favour of Éamon de Valera, who had fought in the Rising. Widely regarded as a national hero, he seemed the obvious choice to lead Sinn Féin. Enthusiasm for the party was at a high, and in the 1918 election, it won 73 of Ireland's 105 parliamentary seats.

The Sinn Féin MPs did what they had pressurised all Irish MPs to do. Refusing to take their seats in Westminster, they invited all Irish MPs to form the First Dáil in Dublin in January 1919. Even as the Dáil held its first meeting in the Round Room of Dublin's Mansion House, the first shots of the Anglo-Irish War were fired. The entire country descended into violence, political concerns took a back seat and Sinn Féin and the Dáil were overshadowed by the activities of the Irish Republican Army (IRA).

Colourised photograph of Bulmer Hobson.

Colourised photograph of Arthur Griffith.

Construction of the *Titanic* commenced in 1909 at the Harland & Wolff shipyard in Belfast. The ship was to be the largest moveable manmade object in the world, and reports of its luxury and opulence preceded its completion. Referred to as the 'Millionaire's Special', the ship's heavily publicised maiden voyage attracted British nobility, members of American society and industrialists. The journey began at Southampton, England, on 10 April 1912. It stopped in Cherbourg, France, to pick up additional passengers and sailed on to Queenstown (now Cobh) in Cork to board the final 123. At 1.30 p.m. on 11 April, the *Titanic* departed Cork for New York City, with an estimated 2,224 people on board. The winter of 1912 had been very mild, and large amounts of ice had broken loose in the Arctic. On 14 April, the *Titanic* received five different ice warnings, but Captain Edward Smith was not overly concerned. The ship steamed ahead. That night the wireless operator received a sixth ice warning, but the message wasn't forwarded to the captain.

At 11.40 p.m. the lookout in the crow's nest spotted an iceberg dead ahead. He notified the bridge, and the ship was turned hard to port. It tried to reverse direction, but it was too large and was moving too fast. The iceberg breached the starboard side and water poured in. Just seconds later, one of the greatest maritime disasters in history began to unfold. The 'practically unsinkable' ship sank within two hours. The lifeboat provision was inadequate (although it exceeded the regulations then in force), and a response to the ship's distress calls by the RMS *Carpathia,* among others, came too late to save those who were stranded in an icy sea. Within hours, over 1,500 lives were lost in one of the deadliest maritime disasters in peacetime.

The iceberg that sank the *Titanic.*

A visitor centre, the Titanic Experience, is located in the Cobh offices of the White Star company, the owner of the ship.

On 31 March 2012, a second Titanic Experience, a beautifully designed immersive visitor centre, opened its doors in Belfast, the *Titanic*'s birthplace.

Artist's impression of the sinking of the *Titanic*.

James Connolly was born in Edinburgh in 1868 to a poor immigrant family from Ireland. He grew up in poverty and joined the British Army at the age of 14. While stationed in Ireland he saw at first hand the overcrowded living conditions in the cities, especially Dublin and Belfast. Families of five or six were living in a single room in houses that often contained more than 100 tenants. He could see that the workers were being sucked dry by their employers.

While Connolly was in the army he discovered the works of Karl Marx and was won over by his teaching. He became a socialist campaigner when he left the army and founded the Irish Socialist Republican Party in Dublin in 1896. At the time Ireland wasn't yet ready to embrace his socialist ideas, and he left for America in 1903. In 1910 he returned to Ireland as a union organiser for the Irish Transport and General Workers' Union in Belfast, which had been founded by James Larkin. Connolly helped organise several successful union actions, and he founded the Irish Workers' Textile Union.

In 1913, Larkin and Connolly worked together for a better pay deal for the tram workers of Dublin. They got nowhere with the United Tramway Company, so they organised a tram strike during the annual Dublin Horse Show, one of Ireland's most important social events. The situation escalated and, before long, almost 25,000 people were out of work, either striking or locked out of their workplaces by their employers. The event became known as the Dublin Lockout.

When Larkin and Connolly were arrested, a street battle between police and protesters left two dead and hundreds wounded. Although the strike failed, Connolly remained in Dublin, organising the Irish Citizen Army – a small, highly trained and well-armed militia, set up to protect workers from police violence. In early 1916, the military council of the IRB invited Connolly and his army to join their planned rebellion.

Street unrest during the Dublin Lockout.

By August 1914, tensions in Ireland had reached fever pitch. On 18 September, the Home Rule bill was presented for the third consecutive year, and this time the House of Lords couldn't veto it. In the north of Ireland, Sir Edward Carson led his Unionists in the formation of the Ulster Defence Force, an army willing to fight against Home Rule. In the south, nationalists under John Redmond were organising the Irish Volunteers.

On 4 August 1914 the United Kingdom of Great Britain and Ireland declared war on Germany. Carson offered Britain the services of the Ulster Defence Force, and John Redmond, to keep in the good graces of the government so that Home Rule wouldn't be killed off, also pledged his Irish Volunteers. For the moment, the European war had de-escalated the tension in Ireland. On 18 September 1914, the Home Rule Act became law, but was suspended because of the war.

Colourised photograph of Sir Edward Carson.

Colourised photograph of John Redmond.

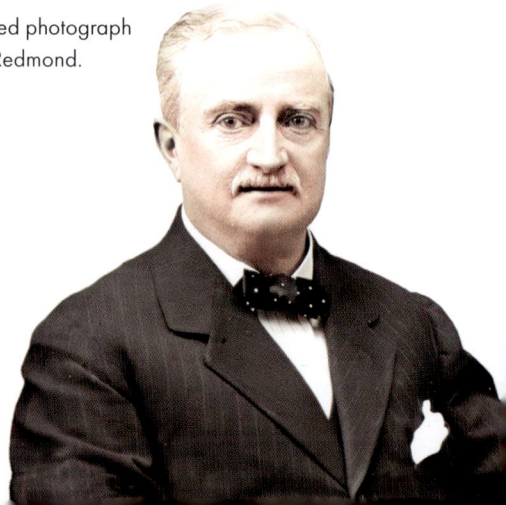

The Irish fought loyally for the British, continuing to volunteer throughout the war, and their families felt betrayed by their own people when the Rising began in 1916. For this reason the Rising received hardly any popular support at the outset. In 1918, running out of new recruits, the British government mooted the desperate idea of conscription in Ireland. It was a step too far, and the idea was dropped after strong opposition from both the leaders of the Catholic Church and Sinn Féin.

By the end of the war in 1918, over 200,000 Irishmen had taken up arms for Britain. Around 30,000 of them had lost their lives, but their sacrifice has never really been acknowledged, and their fate has been overshadowed by that of the heroes of the Easter Rising. Many believed that the Irish who fought for Britain had fought the wrong war in the wrong place.

BE **ONE** OF THE **300,000**

ENLIST **TO-DAY**

and have it to say **YOU** HELPED TO BEAT The **GERMANS**

GO TO THE RECRUITING OFFICER AND **JOIN AN IRISH REGIMENT**

British recruitment poster

By 1916, the sight of Irish Volunteers marching and parading through the streets to support Home Rule was a familiar one. They didn't appear to represent any kind of threat and they were tolerated by the British authorities. However, by now the Irish Volunteers had been infiltrated by the IRB. Under the command of Pádraig Pearse, the IRB took over the militia's operations and began to hatch plans for a rebellion.

One of the main obstacles faced by the plotters was a lack of arms and munitions. The IRB used any means possible to obtain weapons and succeeded in negotiating an arms shipment from Germany, with whom Britain was at war. James Connolly, with his well-trained and -equipped Irish Citizen Army, was persuaded to join forces with the IRB. The uprising was scheduled for 23 April 1916 – Easter Sunday.

The insurgents received a devastating blow on 22 April, when the Royal Navy intercepted the vessel carrying the German arms shipment. The captain scuppered his ship, and the entire cargo of thousands of weapons was lost. It was a bad start.

On Easter Monday, 24 April, the rebels managed to gain control of parts of the city of Dublin, but once the British army had recovered from its surprise, it began to mount a vigorous defence. The rebels were overwhelmed, outgunned by the British, who blasted the rebel positions around the city with long-range artillery fire. The city was on fire. A week into the rising, on 29 April, Pádraig Pearse decided to surrender, to prevent further harm to the city and its residents.

Public opinion had been outraged by the events of Easter Week – with many Irishmen fighting for Britain in the First World War people tended to side with the British, especially in view of the destruction of parts of the capital city. However, the executions of the leaders of the rising provoked a shift in public opinion. Before the firing squads had finished their grisly work, the men who had been reviled just weeks before were being hailed as martyrs.

Colourised photograph of
the destruction at the GPO.

Although the British executed the leaders of the Easter Rising in 1916, they spared the rank and file of the Irish Volunteers and, by 1917, they had regrouped. Now outlawed, they went underground. The First Dáil was established in early 1919, and one of the leaders of the Irish Volunteers, Cathal Brugha, was named Minister of Defence. Many people therefore assumed that the Irish Volunteers would become the official army of the new republic and began referring to the group as the Irish Republican Army (IRA).

However, there was no connection between the Irish Volunteers and Sinn Féin, and their loyalty could not therefore be assumed. While there were some in the Irish Volunteers who were enthusiastic about their new status, others were less so, particularly those cells that were controlled by the highly secretive IRB. When the Dáil began to debate how to achieve separation from Britain, one group of Irish Volunteers embarked on a campaign of violence to force Britain's hand.

The IRA found a new leader in the ranks of the IRB. Michael Collins, Minister of Finance, was a gifted organiser and strategist who was willing to employ terror to achieve the aims of the group. In January 1919 he embarked on a campaign against the forces of the British administration, burning down police barracks and tax offices across the country. He formed a special assassination group called 'The Squad', comprising the most brutally efficient IRA members. The Squad, also known as 'the 12 Apostles', targeted high-profile employees of the British administration, including police detectives and high-level civil servants. The violence was soon widespread.

Members of the IRA special service unit known as The Squad, or the 12 Apostles, established as a counter-intelligence and assassination gang in 1920.

As the dust settled on the Easter Rising, it was increasingly referred to in the media as the 'Sinn Féin' Rising.

Sinn Féin's anti-recruitment campaign against the British army when the First World War started made it a natural home for pacifists and anti-war demonstrators. In what was a logical progression, it was conflated with the IRB, which had been responsible for engineering the Rising. The confusion led to a surge in Sinn Féin membership after the failure of the Rising and the execution of its leaders. It was clear that a new radical element was beginning to dominate the organisation, and a party convention was called in October 1917. Arthur Griffith, one of Sinn Féin's founders, stood down as president in favour of Éamon de Valera.

Éamon de Valera had been one of the leaders of the Easter Rising but his death sentence was commuted because of his dual Irish-American citizenship. He was thus the highest-ranking survivor of 1916, and a national hero.

Colourised photogaph of members of the First Dáil Éireann.

In the 1918 election, Sinn Féin won 73 of Ireland's 105 parliamentary seats. The new Sinn Féin MPs then refused to take their seats at Westminster, calling on all Irish MPs to form a Dáil in Dublin instead. The First Dáil met in the Mansion House in Dublin in January 1919. As it turned out, only the Sinn Féin MPs attended, and only half of those were able to, as the others were still in prison. Despite this, the Dáil set about forming the government for the new independent Irish Republic, based upon the proclamation of the Easter Rising, with Éamon de Valera as the first president. As the Dáil was convening its first meetings in Dublin, Minister of Defence Michael Collins's IRA were firing the first shots in the War of Independence.

Colourised photograph of the official public meeting of the Second Dáil in the Mansion House, Dublin, 16 August 1921. At this meeting Éamon de Valera was elected President of the Republic of Ireland.

On 5 April 1913, the *Daily Mail* newspaper offered two prizes aimed at stimulating the development of aviation, the second of which was £10,000 'to the first person who crosses the Atlantic from any point in the United States, Canada or Newfoundland to any point in Great Britain or Ireland in seventy-two hours'. The competition was suspended owing to the outbreak of the Great War but was reopened in 1918.

Two British military pilots, John Alcock and Arthur Whitten Brown, were selected by the Vickers aviation firm as pilot and navigator for their competition entry of a modified Vickers Vimy bomber. At 1.30 p.m. on 14 June 1919, the pair took off from Lester's Field in Newfoundland. It was hoped that they would get as far as London.

The flight was beset by problems. Less than five hours in, the wind-powered electrical generator failed, cutting off all radio contact, intercom and heating. Heavy fog almost resulted in a crash landing at sea. Eventually, the skies cleared sufficiently to allow for navigation by the stars, but then, in the early hours of 15 June they flew into a snowstorm. Despite their instruments and carburettors icing up, and having to endure freezing temperatures without the benefit of their electrically heated flying suits, Alcock and Brown reached Ireland, crash-landing on Derrygimlagh Bog, near Clifden in County Galway, at 8.40 a.m. on 15 June. The flight had lasted 16 hours and 12 minutes.

The airmen received a heroes' welcome; they were greeted by cheering crowds at every train station they passed through en route to Dublin, where they took the boat to Holyhead. There they were greeted by an enormous crowd, and their train to London had an aerial escort. Winston Churchill, Secretary of State for Air, presented them with their prize, and they were knighted a week later by King George V.

Menu cover for a commemorative luncheon sponsored by the *Daily Mail* newspaper for the first non-stop transatlantic flight.

On 21 May 1932, Amelia Earhart, the first woman to fly solo across the Atlantic, landed in Derry after a 15-hour flight.

Alcock and Brown's transatlantic flight in June 1919. Their modified Vickers Vimy crash-landed in a bog near Clifden, County Galway.

Michael Collins

From January 1919 to January 1920, the IRA's campaign of terror paralysed the British administration. Although the Royal Irish Constabulary (RIC) did its best to maintain law and order, they were under regular attack and their numbers contracted, due to death, injury and an understandable reluctance to join up. In early 1920 Britain began recruiting and shipping a new police force to Ireland. Made up of unemployed former squaddies, the force was soon known as the Black and Tans, a reference to the mismatched colours of their uniforms.

The new force quickly made its presence felt. The Black and Tans were completely undisciplined and were as ruthless as the IRA. The war soon settled into a pattern of attrition, with assassinations carried out by the IRA provoking indiscriminate and brutal reprisals by the Black and Tans.

21 November 1920 was one of the darkest days of the conflict. It all began when Michael Collins ordered the murder of a number of suspected British intelligence agents. A series of coordinated attacks across Dublin left at least 14 dead and dozens injured. The RIC then shot two

IRA prisoners that they claimed were attempting to escape. The authorities suspected that some of the IRA gunmen were hiding amongst the spectators at a Gaelic football match in Croke Park, and Black and Tans were deployed to the scene to block the exits and search for the fugitives. Instead, they opened fire on the crowd. Fourteen people were killed, including one of the players, a woman and three children. A further 60 people were wounded.

Bloody Sunday, together with the campaign of terror carried out by the Black and Tans, was an embarrassment to Britain. The government was desperate to end the war.

A member of the Black and Tans stands guard with a machine gun.

The British, led by the Auxiliaries, a paramilitary unit of the RIC, and supported by the Black and Tans, raided Croke Park and started firing five minutes after the match began.

After Bloody Sunday, the violence increased, with IRA 'flying columns' regularly ambushing RIC convoys. Reprisals were indiscriminate and brutal. Things had reached a tipping point.

In December 1920, the British government proposed the Government of Ireland Act, which revived the idea of Home Rule, but divided Ireland in two: the six Protestant counties of Northern Ireland and the remaining 26 counties. Both would have their own internal parliament to decide domestic issues. The act passed easily, but violence between the IRA and the RIC continued in the south, and a small civil war developed in the north between the Catholics and Protestants.

King George V decided to travel to Belfast for the opening of the new Northern Ireland Parliament. In his address, he appealed 'to all Irishmen to pause … and join in making for the land which they love a new era of peace, contentment and good will'. His speech echoed across the island and, a few weeks later, a truce was called.

De Valera agreed to send a delegation to London to work out a lasting peace. He despatched a team led by Arthur Griffith and Michael Collins, with orders to accept only a treaty that included either a full break from the British Empire or full unity for Ireland. On 6 December 1921, after two months of negotiations, the Irish delegates signed the Anglo-Irish Treaty, which divided the country into six northern counties and 26 southern counties, and established the Irish Free State as a dominion of the British Empire. When the delegation returned to Ireland they were lambasted by de Valera and other Irish nationalists. Most of them were incensed, less by partition than by the retention of the requirement to take an oath to the monarch. The Dáil ratified the treaty, ending the war, but the peace was short-lived.

The scene inside the Oak Room at the Mansion House, Dublin, during the formal ratification of the Irish Treaty, January 1922. Arthur Griffith is seated on the left (centre) wearing glasses and Michael Collins is facing the speaker (bottom left).

By the dawn of the 20th century, it had become clear that several counties within Ulster considered themselves more British than Irish, and were prepared to fight to remain part of the United Kingdom.

When the question of Home Rule came up again in 1912, one British MP proposed that any new Home Rule bill should not apply to the counties of Antrim, Armagh, Down or Londonderry. Within a few years, the debate centred on the question of whether a separate Northern Ireland should be composed of six or nine counties and whether this division should become permanent. In September 1912, organised by the leader of the Ulster Unionists, Sir Edward Carson, almost 500,000 Ulster men and women

In 1913, the Unionists formed the Ulster Volunteer Force (UVF), vowing to resist any attempts by the British Government to impose Home Rule on Ulster.

signed a covenant opposing Home Rule. The following year, the Unionists formed a militia, the Ulster Volunteer Force (UVF). Home Rule was suspended during the First World War and the question of partition was temporarily dropped.

In the north, the War of Independence was a local civil war – Protestants took the opportunity to try to drive out their Catholic neighbours, and the Catholics retaliated. In 1920 the Government of Ireland Act created a separate Northern Ireland, consisting of the counties of Antrim, Armagh, Down, Londonderry, Fermanagh and Tyrone.

However, the Irish Free State quickly descended into civil war and the IRA withdrew from the north to concentrate on the south. This provided Northern Ireland with the opportunity to consolidate its position, and it had achieved a reasonable degree of stability by the time the Civil War came to a conclusion.

Sir Edward Carson

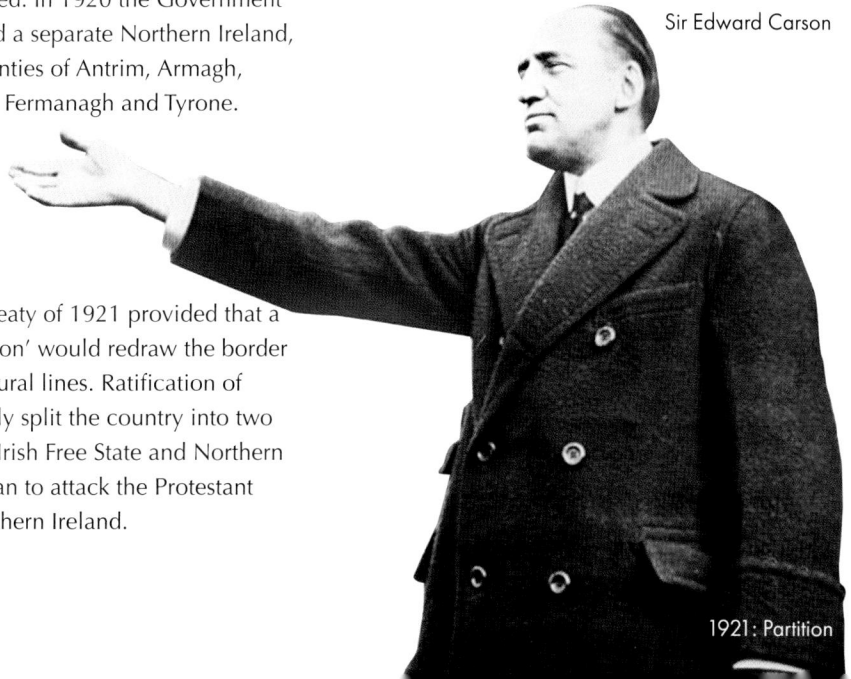

The Anglo-Irish Treaty of 1921 provided that a 'Boundary Commission' would redraw the border on religious and cultural lines. Ratification of the treaty immediately split the country into two separate states – the Irish Free State and Northern Ireland. The IRA began to attack the Protestant infrastructure in Northern Ireland.

When the Anglo-Irish Treaty was ratified by the Dáil, de Valera resigned and was replaced by Arthur Griffith. Britain didn't recognise the Dáil so a new provisional government was set up in Ireland with Michael Collins as the chairman. The British handed over Dublin Castle, the seat of their administration in the country, and left.

The IRA operated from distinct cells, and many of them refused to accept the treaty. They set up headquarters in some of Dublin's buildings, including the centre of the judicial system, the Four Courts. Meanwhile, aided by the British, Michael Collins formed a new Free State Army. On 22 June 1922, the IRA brought their fight to England, murdering Field Marshall Sir Henry Wilson outside his house in London. The British threatened to revoke the treaty unless Collins dealt with the IRA.

Free State soldiers stationed themselves around the IRA strongholds in Dublin and Collins called on them to surrender. When they refused, he opened fire, routing them from their hideouts. Led by Liam Lynch, the IRA retreated into the mountains and began to fight a guerrilla war.

By then the country was tired of war and disruption and this time the IRA had little popular support. Most people just wanted peace and normality and they gave their support to the new Free State. The IRA cells were gradually isolated and then destroyed. On 10 April 1923, Liam Lynch was encircled by Free State troops and was killed. The conflict was at an end. On 30 April, the soldiers of the IRA surrendered their arms and melted into the landscape.

The Civil War erupted because of ideological differences and an unwillingness to compromise. Almost 1,000 people lost their lives, including one of the treaty negotiators and the first chairman of a free Irish state, Michael Collins.

Liam Lynch

Republican prisoners captured during an attack being
marched to Cork Jail for detention.

Michael Collins had fought alongside Pearse and Connolly at the GPO during the 1916 Rising, but was spared execution because the British didn't regard him as one of the leaders. After a short time in prison, he joined Sinn Féin, ran for election and won a seat as MP for South Cork. Along with the other Sinn Féin MPs, he refused to sit in the Westminster parliament, and joined the rest of the Sinn Féin deputies in forming the First Dáil.

As soon as he had put his name to the 1921 Anglo-Irish Treaty, Collins stated that he had signed his own death warrant. He knew that the treaty would be badly received in some quarters in Ireland, but he believed that it was a first step and gave Ireland the best possible chance to eventually achieve full independent statehood.

After the ratification of the treaty, the new government of the Irish Free State elected Collins

The last known photograph of Michael Collins and his aide, Major General Emmett Dalton, taken in Bandon by 20 year-old Agnes Hurley, hours before his death.

as its first chairman. Having set up a Free State Army, he led the fight against the IRA republicans who were threatening to plunge the new state into anarchy.

On 22 August 1922, as Collins was returning from an inspection tour, his convoy was ambushed by a group of IRA gunmen. Collins ordered his men to return fire. During the altercation, he took a bullet to the head. It tore through his skull, killing him instantly. His men brought his body to Dublin, where it lay in state for three days in Dublin City Hall. Tens of thousands of mourners paid their respects.

Today, Michael Collins is regarded both as a hero who advanced the cause of Irish statehood, and as a traitor who colluded with the British in the division of the island of Ireland.

The assassination of Michael Colllins.

The interment of Michael Collins. A line of officers in the Free State Army salute. The figure in the foreground is the gravedigger.

On 6 November 1924, the Boundary Commission set up under the terms of the Anglo-Irish Treaty to determine the boundary between the Irish Free State and Northern Ireland met for the first time. It was chaired by Richard Feetham, a South African lawyer, with Eoin MacNeill representing the Irish Free State and J.R. Fisher, a Unionist newspaper editor from Belfast, delegated by the British government to represent Northern Ireland, whose government refused to cooperate with the Commission.

It had been anticipated that the boundary would be redrawn along cultural and religious lines, and in the course of their information-gathering, the Commission discovered that a large part of the population of Northern Ireland identified strongly as Catholic, and hoped that they would be joining the Free State. However, one of the clauses in the Anglo-Irish Treaty stipulated that the state of Northern Ireland had to remain economically viable – transferring large amounts of territory to the Free State would have undermined this. In a compromise that would have satisfied no one, the Commission intended to recommend quite small transfers, in both

directions. Its findings were leaked to the press, and the Commission collapsed. Ultimately, in order to keep the peace and prevent the outbreak of yet another conflict, the governments of the United Kingdom, Northern Ireland and the Irish Free State signed a three-way agreement in 1925,

Map of the Irish Boundary Commission changes from the *Morning Post*, 1925.

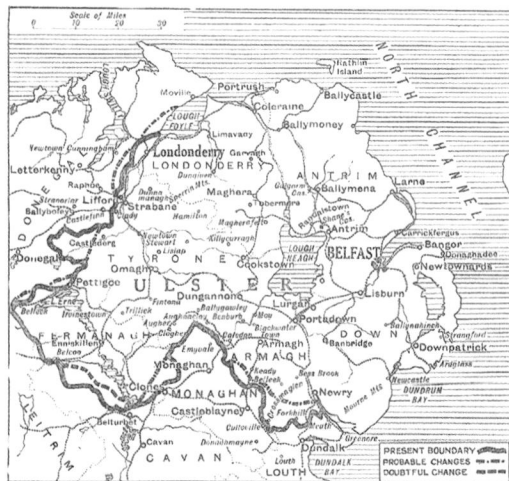

THE BOUNDARY POSITION

Colourised photograph of the Irish Boundary Commission's first sitting in Ireland, Thursday, 11 December 1924. Second from left: Mr J.R. Fisher; centre: Mr Justice Feetham; second from right, Dr Eoin MacNeill.

confirming the border largely as it stood. From the Free State perspective it was a trade-off, whereby its liability for its share of the UK public debt was cancelled in return for agreeing to accept the border more or less as it was.

Since 1925, Northern Ireland has remained separate from the rest of Ireland and has been part of the United Kingdom. The debate on reunification is ongoing.

When Arthur Griffith and Michael Collins died in 1922, William Cosgrave, a former Volunteer and 1916 Rising veteran, took over as the leader of the pro-Treaty faction. In 1923, he formed a new political party, Cumann na nGaedheal. He intended that this 'party of the Irish' would support the democracy that had been set out in the terms of the Anglo-Irish Treaty. Later that year, Cosgrave called a general election, which Cumann na nGaedheal won. De Valera's Sinn Féin was now out of government.

Cumann na nGaedheal had a daunting task. The infrastructure of the country had been undermined during the fighting of the Rising, the War of Independence and the Civil War. Railways, bridges and buildings needed to be repaired and rebuilt. For the first time, a central government would run everything from Dublin rather than London. A new system of education would have to be established, a proper police force would have to be set up and a new legal system introduced. Because most of Ireland's industry was located in Ulster, industries would have to be set up in the Free State to establish a proper industrial base and make the country competitive.

Cosgrave's style of government was slow and cautious, but he succeeded in building a good economic base for the country. One of his major initiatives was the building of the Shannon Hydroelectric Scheme, to provide power to the young nation. However, despite his success, after 10 years people wanted change. De Valera was poised to give it to them.

Still considered a hero by many for his leadership in the Easter Rising, de Valera had broken away from Sinn Féin, forming his own political party, Fianna Fáil, literally meaning 'Soldiers of Destiny', in March 1926. This new party, which comprised large numbers of former Sinn Féin supporters and some of the less radical anti-Treaty voters, would change the face of politics in Ireland.

Political poster for Fianna Fáil.

FIANNA FAIL
(Republican Party)

EAMON de VALERA

will address a Public Meeting of

THE CITIZENS OF DUBLIN

ON

Sunday, May 16th, 1926,

At 3.30 p.m.

LA SCALA THEATRE.

P. J. RUTTLEDGE, T.D.,

WILL ALSO SPEAK.

Colourised photograph of members of the Fianna Fáil
party in 1927, including Éamon de Valera, Constance
Markiewicz, Frank Aiken and Seán Lemass.

In 1925, after a brief test broadcast on 14 November, a Wireless Exhibition was held in Dublin's Mansion House to introduce the population to the benefits of radio broadcasting and to encourage them to buy radio sets. On New Year's Day 1926, Dublin radio station 2RN was launched, marking the beginning of official radio broadcasting in Ireland. Before this, while Ireland had many 'wireless' enthusiasts, listening to radio broadcasts was illegal. BBC radio (the British service had been set up three years previously) broadcasts were relayed to the Mansion House exhibition, providing a taste of what was to come.

Although programming in the early days of radio broadcasting in Ireland was low in quantity and patchy in quality, the introduction of radio was one of the most exciting developments in the new state. On 29 August 1926, 2RN broadcast the first ever coverage of a field game in Europe, the All-Ireland hurling semi-final between Kilkenny and Galway at Croke Park.

Radio provided the opportunity for instant news dissemination directly into people's homes, and was a potential source of entertainment during the long dark evenings of the rural winter.

Initially, listeners in Cork were unable to tune in to 2RN, so a second station, 6CK, was set up in 1927. 2RN and 6CK merged in 1932 as Radio Athlone, when a high-powered transmitter was set up in Athlone to relay the proceedings of the International Eucharistic Congress that was held in Ireland that year. It was officially renamed Raidió Éireann in 1938. In 1939 it became subject to censorship under the Emergency Powers Act, 1939.

Raidió Éireann was cut loose from direct government control in 1960 when a new broadcasting authority was established. In 1973 the studios were moved from Dublin's GPO, where they had been housed since 1928, to a new radio centre at Montrose in Donnybrook. RTÉ Radio now operates four separate stations, including one Irish language channel, covering news, current affairs, sport, classical and popular music, and the arts.

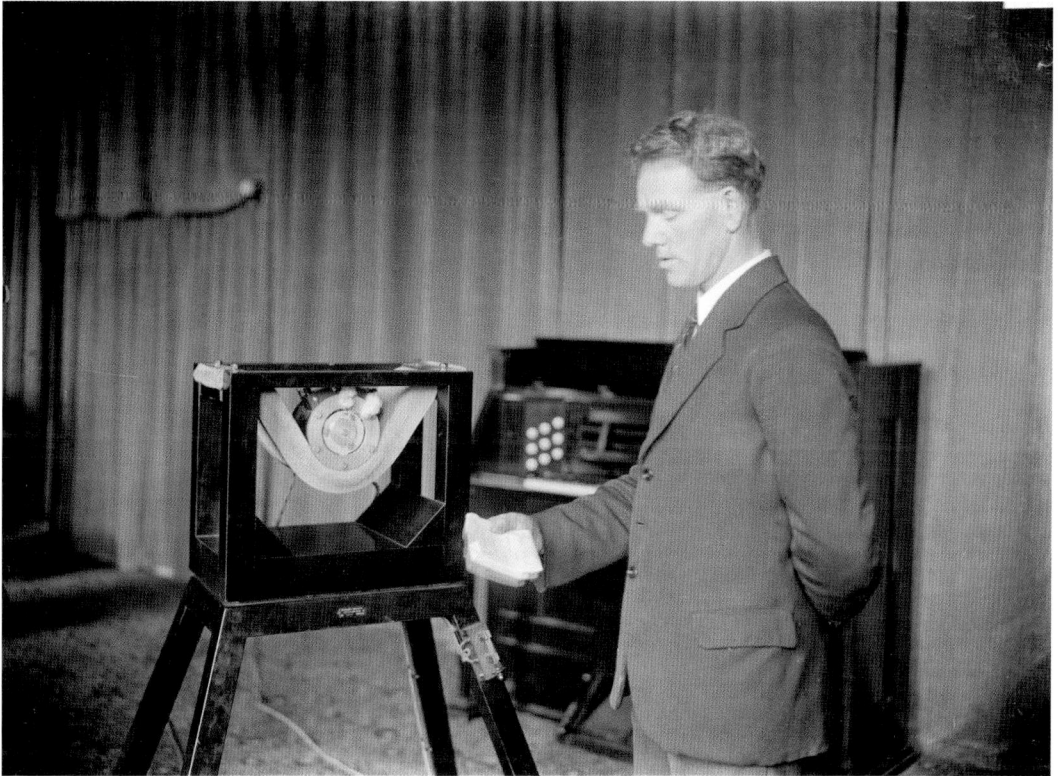

Séamus Hughes, the first full-time radio announcer on 2RN (later renamed Raidió Éireann and subsequently RTÉ Radio), reading an announcement c.1926. The piece of equipment beside him is a 'meat-safe' microphone, so called because of the metal cage protecting the microphone and its similarity to a domestic meat safe. Hughes was appointed full-time station announcer at 2RN in 1925.

From 1896, when the modern Summer Olympic Games held its first edition in Athens, until 1920, Irish athletes competed in the Games in a team that represented Great Britain and Ireland. In 1924 the International Olympic Committee (IOC) formally recognised Ireland as an independent nation, and a team representing the country has competed at the Summer Olympic Games since then (at the 1924 Paris Games the two medals won for Ireland were awarded to Jack B. Yeats and Oliver St John Gogarty in the Olympic Arts and Literature division), and in the Winter Games since 1992. The first winner of a gold medal for Ireland was Patrick O'Callaghan, at the 1928 Amsterdam Olympics, for the hammer throw. He was self-trained and funded his own travel to the games. His expenses for attending the Los Angeles Games in 1932, at which he retained his title, were covered by a church-gate collection.

Since 1924, Ireland has participated in every Summer Olympic Games except the 1936 Berlin edition, which the country boycotted because of a ruling restricting the jurisdiction of the Irish Olympic Council to the territory of the Free State. Ireland has sent teams to the Winter Games since 1992 (with the exception of the Lillehammer Games in 1994). The country's athletes have won a total of 42 medals – 15 gold, 10 silver and 17 bronze – almost half of them for boxing, and Ireland ranks 51st in terms of medals awarded.

The 2024 Summer Games marked Ireland's centenary of participation, and it was the country's most successful participation, with a total haul of seven medals, four of them gold, for swimming, gymnastics, rowing and boxing.

Irish poet Oliver St John Gogarty, by Sir William Orpen.

Patrick O'Callaghan (1906–1991) was an Irish athlete and double Olympic gold medallist. He was the first athlete from Ireland to win an Olympic medal under the Irish rather than the British flag.

Daniel Wiffen won gold in the 800-metre freestyle 24 hours after Mona McSharry's bronze in the 100-metre breaststroke at the 2024 Summer Olympics.

Electricity was introduced to Ireland in 1880 when the first public electric street light was installed on Prince's Street, Dublin. The Dublin Electric Power Company was set up to provide public street lighting throughout the city. The power was provided by three coal-fired power plants. In 1927 the Electricity Supply Board (ESB) was established to bring electricity to the whole country. In 1925 the Irish government under W.T. Cosgrave had launched an ambitious project to build a hydroelectric power plant on the River Shannon. It was constructed by the German engineering firm Siemens-Schukert under the lead of Irish engineer Thomas McLaughlin, who had persuaded the government that it was a worthwhile and necessary investment in the future of the country.

It was a huge undertaking. Almost 100 kilometres of railway were built to carry materials to the site. Excavations to prepare the site removed 7.5 million cubic metres of earth and 1.25 million cubic metres of rock. At the height of construction, over 5,000 workers were employed. The station cost £5.2 million to build.

Ardnacrusha was opened on 22 July 1929 and was officially commissioned in October that year. Siemens had also built a national electricity grid, and power was brought along 3,400 kilometres of power lines to feed into the grid. Two long-distance lines brought power to Dublin and Cork. By 1937, 'the scheme' was supplying 87 per cent of the country's electricity needs. Access to electricity eventually improved social infrastructure and increased employment opportunities, but it took a long time to connect the entire country.

At the time of its construction Ardnacrusha was the most powerful hydroelectric power station in the world. It was overtaken in 1935 by the Hoover Dam in the US, construction on which started the year after Ardnacrusha was commissioned. In 2002 the American Society of Civil Engineers designated Ardnacrusha an Engineering Milestone of the 20th century.

Construction of the main dam and canal in 1925.

Éamon de Valera's new Fianna Fáil party would dominate Irish politics for most of the 20th century. In the 1932 election the party won 72 seats, and de Valera formed a new minority government.

Cosgrave had been a conservative leader, aiming, above all, to promote stability in the new state. De Valera now led Ireland in a period of radical restructuring and separation from Great Britain, convinced that weakening the links between Britain and the Free State would be beneficial. The first thing he did was abolish the Oath of Allegiance to the British crown, a sticking point that had earlier kept members of Sinn Féin from taking their seats in the British Parliament. Then he decided to withhold the land annuities owed to Britain under the 1903 Land Act, which had provided for loans to tenants so that they could buy out their landlords. Britain retaliated by placing a 20 per cent duty on two-thirds of their imports from the Free State. Ireland responded in kind, placing high tariffs on imports from Britain, the first salvo in the 'Economic War'. De Valera hoped that reducing imports from Britain would stimulate Irish industry and make the country self-sufficient. Instead, he faced the wrath of farmers, business owners and ordinary workers, who saw their livelihoods drying up. In 1938 de Valera relented and paid the British £10 million to settle their differences. Part of the deal was the ending of the British occupation of the 'treaty ports' (the naval military bases still used by Britain under the terms of the Anglo-Irish Treaty). The following year, when Britain declared war on Germany, it would have reason to regret giving up the right to use those ports.

Politician and member of Cumann na nGaedheal, W.T. Cosgrave, c.1930.

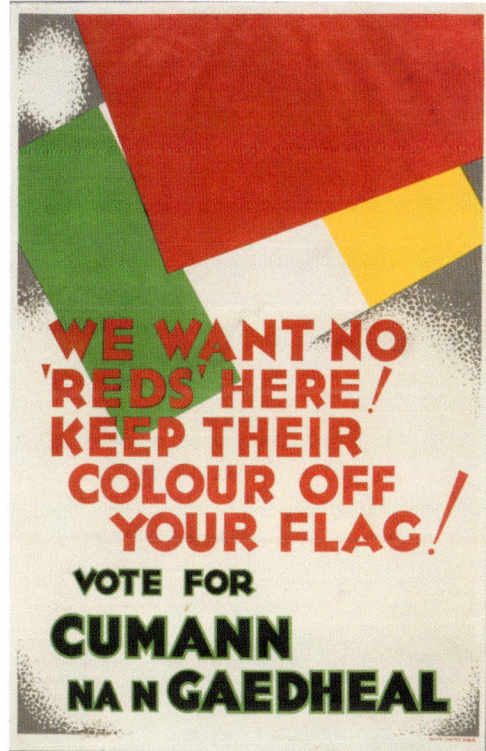

Two election posters by Cumann
na nGaedheal from 1932.

In 1932 religious devotion in Ireland was at its height, and news of a forthcoming International Eucharistic Congress was greeted with passionate enthusiasm by the largely Catholic population of three million. It would be the largest eucharistic congress of the 20th century. Dublin was chosen as the host and the theme of the Congress was a commemoration of the 1,500th anniversary of St Patrick's mission to Ireland. Early Christian Ireland was heavily represented in the decoration of the city. The Congress, in many ways, was a showcase for a new Ireland.

The weather smiled on the Congress, which was held from 22–26 June, and just over 1.5 million people attended the huge outdoor masses. Dublin was decorated with banners, bunting, garlands and light displays. Seven luxury ocean liners, housing just a handful of the 20,000 visitors to the Congress, were moored in Dublin Port. The short-lived ceremonial cavalry unit, the Blue Hussars, had their first public outing. Internationally renowned Irish tenor (and papal count) John McCormack gave an unforgettable performance of 'Panis Angelicus' at the High Mass that closed the proceedings. A radio station was set up in Athlone that was powerful enough to relay the proceedings and a live broadcast by Pope Pius XI across the nation.

Hosting the event suited de Valera's purposes. The Church had excommunicated him for his support of the republican side in the Civil War and he was keen to burnish his Catholic credentials. His high profile during the event – mixing comfortably with Catholic prelates and dignitaries and making an impressive trilingual speech at the state reception in Dublin Castle – left no one in any doubt about his loyalties.

The jubilation engendered by the Congress had another by-product – it confirmed the northern Protestant view that the populations of the north and south were fundamentally different and that partition was the only option.

Pope Pius XI reading his message to the International Eucharistic Congress in 1932.

Benediction on O'Connell Bridge, the Eucharistic Congress, Dublin, June 1932.

Aer Lingus was founded by the Irish government in 1936. The airline was registered on 22 May, and its first aircraft, a six-seater De Havilland biplane, a DH84 Dragon, was delivered four days later. It was registered under the name *Iolar*, meaning 'eagle'. The airline's first passenger flight, from Baldonnell airfield in Dublin to Whitchurch airport in Bristol, took place on 27 May. Within a few weeks, the Isle of Man was added as a route. By September, with the purchase of another aircraft, the network was extended to London.

Aer Lingus was established as the national air carrier in 1937 and an airport management company, Aer Rianta, was set up. At the beginning of 1940, Aer Lingus moved its operations to a new Dublin airport at Collinstown.

The outbreak of the Second World War meant that flights were stripped back and regular service didn't resume until November 1945. In 1946, Paris became the airline's first European destination. Cabin crew were introduced in the late 1940s and it was decided to call all the planes in the fleet after Irish saints. In 1958 the airline inaugurated its transatlantic routes, to New York and Boston.

With the dawn of the jet age, the airline bought three Boeing 720s for the New York and Boston routes and began to upgrade the entire fleet. The shamrock replaced the Irish tricolour on the tails of the planes. In 1977 the first female pilot was recruited.

In 1988 Aer Lingus celebrated its golden jubilee, but difficult times lay ahead. After the Gulf crisis in the 1990s, the air travel sector slumped and the Irish airline almost collapsed. A restructuring plan rescued it from the brink. After 9/11 there was a slump in transatlantic air travel and Aer Lingus was forced to go down the low-fare route. It was a profitable move and in 2006 the airline was privatised. As it approaches its centenary of operations, it remains an instantly recognisable global ambassador for Ireland.

The Tusker Rock tragedy

On 24 March 1968, Aer Lingus flight 712 crashed off County Wexford on a flight from Cork to London, killing all 61 passengers and crew.

A two-year investigation found no cause for the crash, but an Irish government investigation in 2002 concluded that the plane probably broke up in mid-air due to a structural failure of the port tail plane, caused by corrosion, metal fatigue or a bird strike.

A DH84 Dragon, repainted in the livery of Aer Lingus' original aircraft, *Iolar*.

A postcard of a 1960s Aer Lingus jet being refueled at Dublin Airport.

On 25 October 1922, the Constitution of the Irish Free State, granting the territory dominion status, was adopted by an Act of Dáil Éireann sitting as a constituent assembly. It was a stepping stone to full independence.

In 1935, de Valera set civil servants the task of constructing a new constitution. In 1937, he put the document to a popular vote. The result was 645,105 for the Constitution and 526,945 against. It was adopted in 1937.

For the southern 26 counties, this signalled the end of over 500 years of British government intervention in Ireland. The new document was built on the foundation of the 1922 Constitution, but gave the country a new name, Éire, and declared the country a sovereign and independent state. It defined Éire as consisting of the entire island of Ireland, but recognised that its authority, for the time being, extended only to the southern 26 counties. The Constitution provided for a new head of government called a taoiseach, deriving from the ancient Irish word for king or chief. A president would be head of state, with far-reaching discretionary powers.

Article 44 of the Constitution accorded a special position to the Catholic Church, and adopted many of its teachings as law. The sale of contraceptives was outlawed and divorce would no longer be legal.

The Constitution is a living document, and can be amended by referendum. The 16th amendment (1996) permitted legislation for the introduction of divorce; the 19th amendment (1998) provided a vehicle for the state to relinquish its claim to sovereignty over the whole island of Ireland; the 34th amendment (2015) provided for the introduction of same-sex marriage; and the 36th amendment (2018) provided for the repeal of the 8th amendment (1983), which had rejected abortion.

A Fine Gael poster used in the Irish constitutional referendum of 1937.

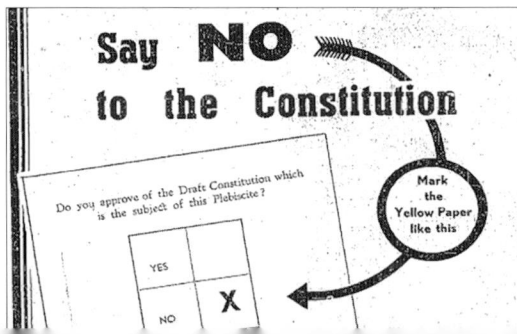

Éamon de Valera

De Valera had been adamant throughout his political career that a complete separation from Britain was necessary for the country. When Britain declared war on Germany in 1939, he declared that Ireland would remain neutral in the conflict. Even when Prime Minister Winston Churchill later offered his support for the reunification of Ireland in return for a wartime alliance, de Valera dug in his heels, determined that Ireland would decide her own destiny. However, Ireland's 'neutrality' was not as cut and dried as it purported to be, and the Republic of Ireland was helpful in many ways to the Allied cause.

De Valera didn't try to prevent people from volunteering in the British armed forces and almost 50,000 Irishmen joined the army, winning hundreds of honours for bravery in battle. Britain's highest military award, the Victoria Cross, was awarded to seven Irishmen.

With so many British workers on military service, the labour force was decimated. Over 200,000 Irish people went to work in Britain, plugging the gap in the British economy that had been left by those who had gone off to fight in the war.

There was never any doubt that Northern Ireland would pitch in during the war. Several key airfields were built there, and from 1942, the US used Northern Ireland as a base from which to plan the invasion of North Africa and to build up troops for the D-Day invasion. More than 300,000 US servicemen were stationed in Northern Ireland during the war.

Londonderry became an important port in the movement of merchant shipping convoys from the US to Britain. The north's usefulness to the war effort inevitably made it a German target. In 1941, German planes bombed Belfast, destroying 56,000 homes and killing approximately 1,000 people. The air raid campaign became known as the 'Belfast Blitz'.

Opposite: The aftermath of bombing in Dublin during the Second World War, with workers searching the wreckage for survivors. An estimated 30–40 people were killed.

Thomas McLaughlin, the instigator of the Ardnacrusha project, believed that rural electrification represented 'the application of modern science and engineering to raise the standard of rural living and to get to the root of the social evil of the "flight from the land"'. When the Ardnacrusha power station commenced operations, 60 per cent of the population lived outside the urban centres that were first connected to electricity. Electrification throughout the countryside was deferred by the outbreak of the Second World War, and the ESB's Rural Electrification Scheme didn't commence until 1946. In January 1947 the first lights of the scheme were switched on in the village of Oldtown, County Dublin.

The first phase of rural electrification lasted almost 20 years, from 1946 to 1965. It was a huge undertaking. Over a million wooden poles and almost 80,000 kilometres of wire were required. There weren't enough trees in Ireland to satisfy the requirements of the project and poles had to be imported from Finland.

Politicians and even priests lobbied heavily for their areas to be connected first, and meetings were held to encourage people to sign up for connection. Householders signed up voluntarily, and those areas with the most takers were serviced first. If one's neighbours weren't interested, and some weren't, for a variety of reasons, the chances of connection were slim. In some cases people signed up but then changed their mind – they were known as 'backsliders'. There was a great deal of poverty in rural Ireland in the 1950s and there were many instances where 'no funds' was cited as a reason for refusal. Although the scheme was heavily subsidised by the state, householders had to pay a connection fee and to have their homes wired. In addition, there were those who were suspicious of change, or who worried that electric wires might ignite their thatched roofs.

By 1965 more than 300,000 homes had been connected to electricity. By 1975, 99 per cent of Irish homes were connected. The scheme was completed in 1977, when the lights finally went on in Black Valley, County Kerry.

The first pole being erected at Kilsallaghan, County Dublin, 5 November 1946.

View of the dam on the River Shannon at O'Briensbridge.

De Valera hoped to create a fully independent, self-sufficient country, free of any outside influence. However, his tariff walls made the island unappealing to foreign investors, who took their business and their money elsewhere. The lack of jobs started a new wave of Irish emigration that drained the country of its youth and vitality.

During the war years, most of these problems had stayed under the radar. People had enough difficulty coping with day-to-day life in the face of shortages. At the time, the huge migration of workers to Britain seemed to be temporary, and it was expected that they'd return to Ireland after the war. However, a large number decided to stay on in Britain after the war, and the trend of outward migration continued.

In the 1948 general election, the issue of emigration brought about Fianna Fáil's downfall. A new coalition government was formed under Taoiseach John A. Costello. Costello pushed through the Republic of Ireland Act, which created the Republic of Ireland as a country outside the British Commonwealth. It had no impact on the economic situation, which continued to worsen.

With very few jobs available to them and deprived of marriage prospects, large numbers of women left Ireland. Most of them headed to Britain, where jobs in professions like nursing offered good salaries and better opportunities for meeting potential husbands. The government discussed drastic measures such as the imposition of a lower age limit for female emigration or even the requirement to pay a large fee to leave the country.

Costello's government failed in 1951 and was replaced by de Valera's Fianna Fáil government. Costello was returned to power again in 1954. The country became caught in a seemingly endless spiral of migration and economic depression. It was estimated that in 1954, only 30 per cent of the Irish population was married. This was the worst marriage rate in Europe at the time.

In 1957, Fianna Fáil once again returned to power. De Valera, by now an old man, resigned in 1959 and Seán Lemass became taoiseach.

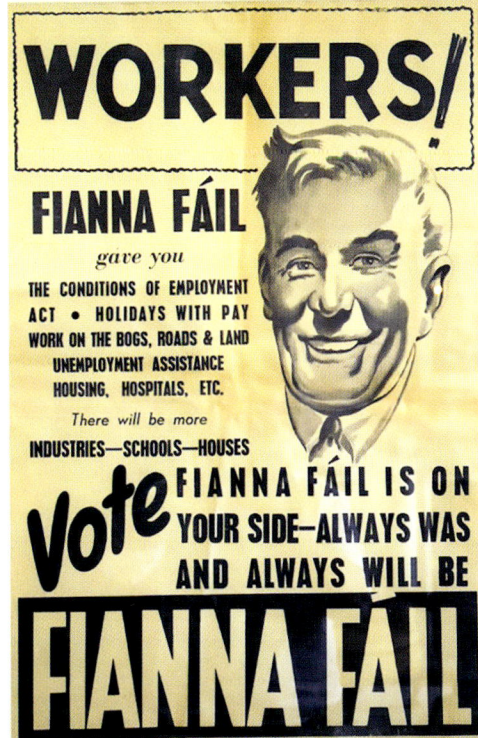

1948 Fianna Fáil election posters.

In the 1948 general election, Fianna Fáil, which had been in office continuously since 1932, lost its majority and was replaced by a coalition government of Fine Gael, the Labour Party, Clann na Poblachta, Clann na Talmhan and the National Labour Party. Dr Noël Browne, a Clann na Poblachta TD, became Minister for Health. In 1947 Fianna Fáil had enacted health legislation, which, among other things, had a plan to address the very high rate of infant mortality in Ireland, by making healthcare free at point of access to mothers and under-16s without means-testing.

Browne, an admirer of Britain's new National Health Service, was eager to implement the 1947 Health Act. In 1950 he submitted the Mother-and-Child Scheme to the Irish Medical Association, which had opposed the 1947 legislation on the grounds that it would open the door to socialised medicine.

More importantly, given the special constitutional position accorded the Catholic Church, the Archbishop of Dublin, John Charles McQuaid, summoned Browne to his palace to read out a letter that was about to be sent to the taoiseach, John A. Costello, stating that the archbishops and bishops 'feel bound by their office to consider whether the proposals are in accordance with Catholic teaching'. There was a concern that doctors who hadn't been trained in Catholic institutions 'may give gynaecological care not in accordance with Catholic principles', and that the scheme might open the floodgates to birth control and abortion.

Browne refused to back down. He had little support from his colleagues, who regarded him as a loner and something of a maverick, and his party leader, Seán MacBride, demanded his resignation. Browne resigned in April 1951. The Mother-and-Child Scheme was never implemented, although free maternity care was eventually provided for in the Health Act of 1953.

Portrait of Noël Browne
(1915–1997), Robert
Ballagh, (b.1943) at the
National Gallery of Ireland.
Browne was a doctor,
politician and campaigner.

When Séan Lemass became taoiseach in 1959, Ireland had been suffering from mass emigration and economic stagnation for more than a decade. Lemass had been active in politics since fighting at the GPO in 1916, and he had the courage and the confidence to bring about the radical change that would begin to turn Ireland's fortunes around.

Lemass had been Minister for Industry and Commerce in the first de Valera government of 1932, the youngest member of the cabinet. He launched a number of state-sponsored enterprises in the 1930s, including the Industrial Credit Company, the Turf Development Board (this would become Bord na Móna), the Irish Sugar Company, the Irish Tourist Board and Aer Lingus. He was a forward- and outward-looking man, with a deep understanding of economics, and he realised that Irish society would have to modernise in order to meet the many challenges of the post-Second World War world. When Fianna Fáil lost the election in 1948 he felt deep frustration at being suddenly out of power, and went as far as to resist the government's establishment of the Industrial Development Authority (IDA) in 1949.

In the sphere of economics, Lemass had been inspired the work of Dr T.K. Whitaker. As Secretary of Finance, Whitaker had produced a paper in 1958 entitled *Economic Development*. This called for a reduction in the counter-productive import duties introduced by de Valera that had been designed to protect the Irish economy. Whitaker saw the persuasion of overseas companies to establish manufacturing in Ireland as the way forward. Lemass immediately adopted Whitaker's policies, implementing the First Programme for Economic Expansion. The abandonment of the principle of protection in favour of inward foreign investment had overwhelmingly successful results. For the next five years the Gross National Product averaged more than 4 per cent growth and emigration dropped to nearly a third of its earlier levels. With hope in the air, Ireland's population began to increase once again.

New taoiseach, Seán Lemass, in 1959.

On 6 April 1960 the Broadcasting Authority Act established a new television service for the Republic of Ireland, and removed broadcasting from the direct control of the government. The Radio Éireann Authority was established, with Eamonn Andrews as its first chairman. RTÉ Television was founded on 1 June, and staff began to move from their Henry Street studios to a new, purpose-built complex at Montrose in Donnybrook in December 1961.

The station was launched on New Year's Eve 1961, with an address by President de Valera. The launch was anticipated by the first issue of a television guide, *The RTV Guide* (now *The RTÉ Guide*). The first programmes to be aired from Montrose were news bulletins – with construction of the new complex ongoing, construction work could sometimes be heard during the news broadcasts. The first weather forecast was broadcast on RTÉ One television on 1 January 1962 after the main evening news. It was presented by Met Éireann meteorologist George Callaghan, who brought the maps and other documents to the studio on his bicycle.

Gay Byrne in 2007.

1962 saw the first broadcast of *The Late Late Show*, hosted by Gay Byrne. It is now the second longest-running television chat show in the world. In 1963 RTÉ provided coverage of US President John F. Kennedy's visit to Ireland. A second channel, now RTÉ Two, went on air in 1978. The 1993 Eurovision Song Contest, held in Millstreet, County Cork, was broadcast by RTÉ. During the interval of the 1994 Eurovision, *Riverdance* was performed for the first time.

RTÉ is a public service broadcasting authority. Reflecting this, the Broadcasting Complaints Commission was set up in 1976, and the RTÉ Audience Council was established in 2006. RTÉ television programmes are available to 99 per cent of residents of Ireland in return for a licence fee, and can also be viewed internationally via a subscription streaming service.

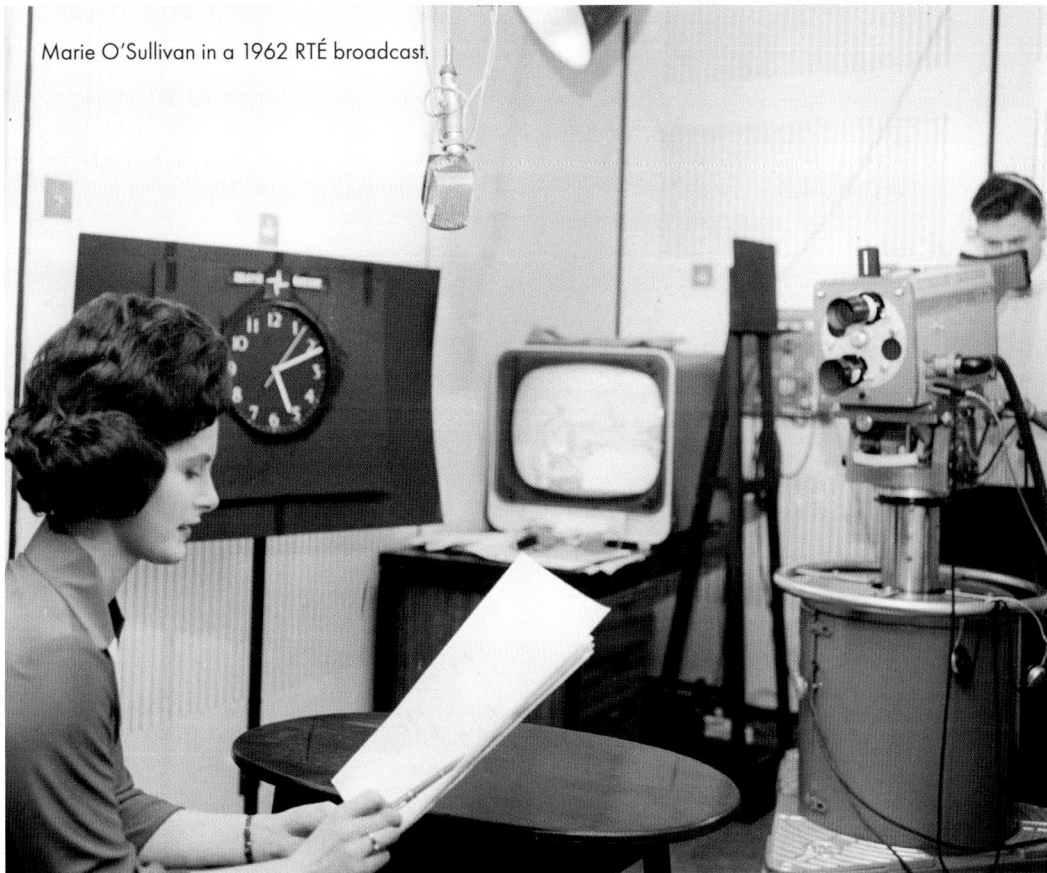

Marie O'Sullivan in a 1962 RTÉ broadcast.

John Fitzgerald Kennedy first visited Ireland at the age of 28 in 1945, as a reporter for Hearst newspapers. On that occasion he interviewed President de Valera. Having been elected to the US Congress, he returned in 1947 with his sister Kathleen. As a US Senator, he stopped off in Ireland briefly in 1955 for a meet-and-greet with Irish leaders that would burnish his Irish-Catholic credentials in the US. He was already being groomed for the US presidency, which he won in 1960 against Richard Nixon in a race that had been too close to call.

Ireland was then a backwater, poor and undeveloped, with high unemployment and a constant stream of emigrants leaving the country in search of a better life. It ranked very low in terms of world importance. In 1963, enjoying an 82 per cent approval rating, President Kennedy embarked on a European tour that would include Ireland, his ancestral home. On 26 June, he flew from Berlin to Dublin on a four-day visit. He was greeted by President de Valera with a welcome address in Irish and English.

The trip was a resounding success, instigating a special relationship between Ireland and the US. It was a whistle-stop tour of the Republic (Kennedy's offer to visit the North was declined), the president receiving a rapturous reception wherever he went. From Dublin he went to New Ross and Dunganstown in County Wexford to visit relatives; to Cork by helicopter, then back to Dublin, to Arbour Hill for the annual 1916 commemoration, and Leinster House, where he addressed the Dáil, the first foreign leader in the history of the state to do so. His speech was broadcast to the nation by the recently established RTÉ television service. He received honorary degrees from both the National University and Trinity College Dublin. He then went on to Galway, Limerick (where he was addressed by Ireland's first female mayor, Frances Condell) and Clare, where he departed from Shannon Airport. Five months later he was dead, gunned down by an assassin in Dallas.

President Kennedy's motorcade in Patrick Street, Cork, 28 June 1963.

1963: JFK visits Ireland | 183

Nelson's Pillar in 1829.

Nelson's Pillar was a 39-metre high granite column topped with a statue of Admiral Horatio Nelson, hero of the Battle of Trafalgar, erected on Sackville Street (now O'Connell Street) in Dublin in 1809. It was constructed with money raised from public subscription. There was some discussion about the best location for the monument. It was thought that it should look out to sea – Howth was mentioned as a possibility – but Sackville Street was chosen in a bid to revive Dublin City's sagging fortunes in the aftermath of the 1800 Act of Union.

A third of Nelson's sailors were from Ireland, about 400 from Dublin, so the pillar was enthusiastically received by the population of the capital. It was a popular tourist attraction from the outset, but, as the years went on, its existence didn't sit easily with the increasing numbers of Irish nationalists. Throughout the 19th century there were calls for it to be removed and replaced with a memorial to a notable Irish person.

Despite the contrarian voices, the pillar survived the establishment of the Irish Free State and the Republic. While it had its detractors, there were those who spoke up for it, including Senator W.B. Yeats.

At 1.30 a.m. on the morning of 8 March 1966, a huge blast destroyed the statue of Nelson. The windows of adjacent shopfronts were blown in and a taxi was destroyed by rubble, but there were no human casualties. At first it was thought that the IRA was responsible, but the group issued a denial and, although there were some arrests, no one was charged. Dublin Corporation issued a 'dangerous building' notice and the stump of the pillar was blown up by the army on 14 March.

In 2000 a man called Liam Sutcliffe confessed to the bombing on RTÉ radio. He was arrested but released without charge.

In 2003, the 120-metre needle-like Spire of Dublin, the Monument of Light, was erected in O'Connell Street on the site of the demolished monument.

The half-demolished Nelson's Pillar on O'Connell Street, Dublin.

When Northern Ireland was created as a separate state, no attempt was made to protect the Catholics that made up a third of the population, and the Protestants took advantage of the situation. They passed laws that made state schools Protestant in all but name, and discrimination against Catholic teachers was facilitated. In those areas where Protestants were in the minority, such as Londonderry, they rigged the electoral system to their advantage.

Most Catholics in the North refused even to acknowledge the existence of the state. Soon, Northern Ireland reverted to a situation where the gun became more important than the rule of law. The IRA established themselves as the defenders of the Catholics, while the ostensibly impartial Royal Ulster Constabulary (RUC) dedicated themselves to protecting Protestant interests.

Despite the increasing tendency towards violence, there were some advances, even for the Catholic population. The education system in Northern Ireland in the 1940s created an educated Catholic middle class which came into its own during the 1960s.

Much of the IRA's funding came from the US, but it wasn't just money that crossed the Atlantic. The Civil Rights Movement, led by Martin Luther King, inspired a group of the new Catholic middle class to form the Northern Ireland Civil Rights Association (NICRA) in 1967. Their aim was to use peaceful protest to overthrow the religious injustice that was inherent in the Northern Irish government.

In 1968, the NICRA organised its first march in Dungannon and gathered 2,500 people in protest. Unfortunately, the IRA and the RUC provided an obstacle to the peaceful nature of these protest marches, and many subsequent marches soon turned into riots. Away from the marches, the violence escalated and terrorism had soon become endemic in the province. Snipers fired on civilians and people had to dig tunnels through their houses and gardens to get to shops and schools. Some Catholic areas became 'no-go' areas for police and military. Murder, beatings and the sound of gunfire were rife.

Derry, 1968, a civil rights demonstration.

By August 1969, the violence in Northern Ireland was spiralling out of control. The security situation was so bad that Britain decided to send in the military to restore some sort of order. At first, Catholics welcomed the soldiers who patrolled their streets, but it soon became clear that the British soldiers didn't know how to deal with the volatile situation with which they were faced. Their heavy-handed attempts to deal with it antagonised the Catholic population who had soon turned against them and towards the IRA.

Internment without trial was introduced in August 1971. Emotions ran high as people were rounded up and detained indefinitely. The NICRA organised a protest march against internment on 30 January 1972. Anticipating violence, British soldiers, who later said that they believed they were under attack by some of the marchers, shot at the crowd of unarmed civilians. The situation became chaotic. Twenty-six people were shot, and 14 died. Many of the victims had been running away when shot, others were injured by rubber bullets or shrapnel, and two were run down by army vehicles. The event borrowed a classic name from an earlier incident at Croke Park in Dublin more than 50 years earlier, in 1920, and it became known as 'Bloody Sunday', or the Bogside Massacre. It had the highest number of killings in a single incident during the entire period of the Troubles. However, Bloody Sunday was just one incident in the most violent year of the conflict – 500 people were killed in the violence that stalked Northern Ireland in 1972.

After the horrific events of Bloody Sunday, the violence escalated again. The Westminster government was concerned that the Northern Irish response would never provide a solution to the worsening situation. Deciding that it needed to step in, Westminster declared Direct Rule over Northern Ireland.

Mural from Bloody Sunday showing Fr Edward Daly waving a white handkerchief, the men behind carrying a wounded man.

The good times that had been generated by the forward-looking polices of the Lemass government didn't last. The growth of the Irish economy during the Lemass years had been aided by a strong British economy, and when this began to crash in the 1960s, it had a dramatic knock-on effect on Irish growth. In the face of this downturn, the Irish continued to look for ways to better their position. In 1963 and 1967 Ireland had applied for membership of the European Economic Community (EEC) but were rebuffed by President de Gaulle of France. In 1969, a new French President, Georges Pompidou, said he wouldn't stand in the way of Irish and British accession, and in 1972 over 80 per cent of the Irish population voted in a referendum to join the EEC (which later evolved into the European Union). Irish membership began officially on 1 January 1973.

Membership of the EEC brought immediate benefits, such as the Common Agricultural Policy (CAP), which granted Ireland farming subsidies and guaranteed higher prices. Ireland also received funding from European social and regional programmes. Roads and infrastructure were upgraded, leading to improved national communications. Unfortunately, the 1970s saw huge fluctuations in world economic markets and a massive spike in the price of oil, both of which caused continuing economic hardship for the population of Ireland.

The situation improved enormously in the late 1980s and early 1990s, leading to the economic phenomenon known as the 'Celtic Tiger'. European funding continued until 2018, by which time Ireland had received more than €40 billion. Today, the country is a net contributor to the European Union (EU) budget.

A first day cover issued to celebrate Ireland's accession to the EEC.

The signing ceremony of the Accession Treaty for Ireland was held on 22 January 1972 in the Egmont Palace, Brussels. In the photo, Taoiseach Jack Lynch (left) and Patrick Hillery, Irish Minister for Foreign Affairs (right) sign the Treaty.

On 29 September 1979, less than a year after his election to the papacy, Pope John Paul II arrived at Dublin Airport to a rapturous welcome. In fact, this began before his plane had even touched down, when the crowd of 1.25 million people assembled for Mass in the Phoenix Park let out a huge roar as the Pope's plane flew overhead. As soon as the Pope stepped onto the airport tarmac, he knelt and kissed the ground, a gesture that would become familiar during his long pontificate.

After saying Mass at the Phoenix Park, the Pope travelled to Drogheda, in the Archdiocese of Armagh, where he led a liturgy for a crowd of 300,000, and issued a plea to those engaging in violence to turn towards peace. The next day, he went to Clonmacnoise, then on to Galway for a youth Mass for 300,000, ending the day at Knock in County Mayo with a Mass for 450,000. His final Mass, for 400,000, was at Limerick. It is estimated that 2.75 million people, out of a population of three million, attended a papal Mass during his visit.

The papal visit took place at a pivotal moment in the history of the Irish Catholic Church. In 1979, Ireland was on the cusp of change, evolving from a land of deep faith to one preoccupied with material advancement. During his visit the Pope prayed that the prosperity to which the people aspired would not cause them 'to forget God or abandon their faith', and asked that 'they would remain faithful in prosperity to the faith they would not surrender in poverty'.

By the time of the next papal visit, that of Pope Francis in 2018, Ireland had changed. Quite apart from the country's new-found prosperity, the Church had been grappling with the scandal of clerical sexual abuse of children and the fallout of its involvement in the Magdalene Laundries from the foundation of the state to the 1990s. Pope Francis's Phoenix Park Mass had a congregation of 152,000, and 45,000 people attended a papal prayer service at Knock shrine.

The Pope's visit drew huge crowds.

Direct rule in Northern Ireland was introduced as a stopgap measure, and Britain realised that a lasting solution to the violence that was tearing the province apart would have to be found. In 1972, William Whitelaw, the British Secretary of State, put forward proposals for power-sharing by all the major political parties in Northern Ireland. A peace conference was held in 1973 to discuss these, and the Sunningdale Agreement was signed in December 1973. The power-sharing executive it established was short-lived – the different parties found it impossible to agree on anything.

The situation worsened and was soon approaching anarchy, with an average of 100 people dying in the Troubles each year for the next two decades. Before long the violence began to spill over to mainland Britain. The IRA had started to bomb targets in England in 1972, the first incident carried out in retaliation for Bloody Sunday. They stepped up their campaign in the 1980s and Prime Minister Margaret Thatcher was targeted by them in the Brighton hotel bombing during the Conservative Party conference of 1984. Realising that unilateral negotiations with the IRA were never going to be productive, Westminster began a consultation process with the Republic of Ireland.

In 1981 Taoiseach Garret FitzGerald had launched a 'constitutional crusade', aimed at making Irish reunification more attractive to the North's Protestants. Relations between Britain and Ireland had been improving, and an inter-governmental council was set up to discuss the situation, particularly the most pressing problem of security. The Irish-American lobby in the US put a lot of pressure on the parties to reach a solution and the talks eventually culminated in the Anglo-Irish Agreement of 1985, signed by Margaret Thatcher and Garret FitzGerald. It provided for meetings between representatives of both governments in the areas of security, legal affairs and cross-border cooperation. Protests by Northern Unionists, furious at Ireland's consultative role in the affairs of Northern Ireland, came to nothing, and the agreement stood.

The Grand Hotel in Brighton following the IRA bomb attack. The photo was taken on the morning of 12 October 1984, some hours after the blast.

Garret FitzGerald (1926–2011).

Margaret Thatcher (1925–2013)

When Mary Robinson was inaugurated as President of Ireland on 3 December 1990, she became the seventh president and the first woman to hold the office. She said that she had been elected by the women of Ireland, who, 'instead of rocking the cradle, rocked the system'.

Robinson had studied law at Trinity College Dublin, at a time when the Catholic Church's discretionary ban on the attendance of Catholics was still in force – she had to apply for a dispensation from the Archbishop of Dublin, John Charles McQuaid, to attend the university. She was called to the Irish Bar in 1967, and won several landmark cases during her career. In 1969, aged 25, she became the youngest Reid Professor of Criminal Law at Trinity. She was elected to Seanad Éireann the same year. She aimed to bring about reform of the law in the areas of contraception, homosexuality and divorce. She campaigned for women to be allowed to serve on juries, a right that was granted in 1976.

Robinson won the Labour nomination for the presidency and ran against Austin Currie for Fine Gael and Brian Lenihan for Fianna Fáil (who was generally regarded as the likely winner).

Fallout from a political scandal reduced Lenihan's appeal and Robinson won the election, the first non-Fianna Fáil candidate to do so. By the time she was halfway through her term of office, her popularity rating was 93 per cent. During her tenure as president she signed bills liberalising contraception, decriminalising homosexuality and legalising divorce.

She resigned from the presidency a few weeks early, in September 1997, to take up an appointment as the United Nations High Commissioner for Human Rights. She was succeeded in the Irish presidency by the second woman to hold the office, Mary McAleese.

Mary Robinson

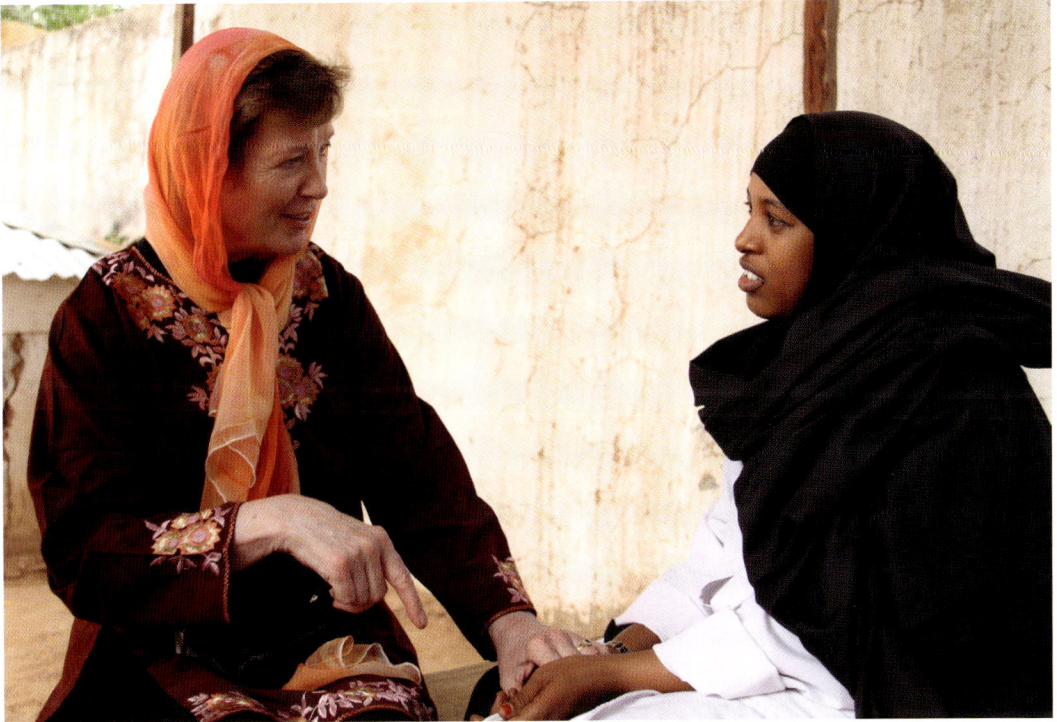

Mary Robinson with healthworker Nadhifa Ibrahim
Mohamed, Dollow, Somalia.

The law in Ireland relating to homosexuality derived from sections 61 and 62 of the Offences against the Person Act 1861, which made sodomy an offence punishable by imprisonment with hard labour. Irish poet and playwright Oscar Wilde, notoriously, had fallen foul of this law in 1895.

Gay rights organisations began to be formed in Ireland in the early 1970s. In 1977, David Norris, a lecturer at Trinity College Dublin and leader of the Campaign for Homosexual Law Reform, took legal proceedings challenging the constitutionality of the legal prohibitions on homosexuality. He argued that the law contravened his implicit right to privacy under the Constitution. In 1980 he lost his case in the High Court and then lost his appeal to the Supreme Court in 1983. He brought his case to the European Court of Human Rights, which ruled in 1985 that the legislation he was challenging contravened the European Convention on Human Rights.

In 1990 the Law Reform Commission recommended the repeal of the relevant legislation, and that the age of consent for both heterosexual and homosexual activity be the same. After a great deal of campaigning and lobbying the Criminal Law (Sexual Offences) Act was passed in 1993, decriminalising homosexual acts between consenting adult men. It had been a long road for David Norris, by now a senator, and all those who had joined him along the way. Speaking at the debate on the legislation, he said, 'This is for me a happy day for my fellow legislators have chosen, as the lawmakers of a free and independent republic, to liberate the gay community from an oppressive, corrupt and deeply damaging law, whose origins are shrouded in the mists of ancient religious prejudice.'

In 2010, the Civil Partnership Act gave LGBT couples rights deriving from their relationships that had previously been denied them, and in May 2015, the population voted overwhelmingly in a referendum to allow for the introduction of same-sex marriage. Ireland thus became the first country in the world to legalise same-sex marriage by popular vote.

Drag queen and gay rights activist Rory O'Neill, known by his stage name Panti Bliss, arrives at the Central Count Centre in Dublin Castle, as votes continue to be counted in the referendum on same-sex marriage.

When Charles Haughey became taoiseach in 1980 he warned the people of Ireland that the economic outlook was tough. His Fianna Fáil government proceeded to make draconian spending cuts. The policy worked. Between 1987 and 1993 GDP rose by 36 per cent, which was almost three times the average rate of growth for the rest of the EU. Suddenly, Ireland, from being one of the poorest countries in Europe, had become a 'Celtic Tiger'. Its young, well-educated, English-speaking population attracted corporations from all over the world.

Between 1995 and 2005, Ireland's industrial production tripled, its exports quadrupled and the disposable income of the average Irish person doubled. With rising prosperity, Ireland grew in confidence.

Having benefited so greatly from EU membership, the country enthusiastically supported the accession of new members to the EU, becoming one of only three countries in the union to continue to allow unrestricted access to migrant workers. The population and ethnic diversity in the country increased as a result. By the year 2000, unemployment in Ireland had dropped below 5 per cent and average living standards were estimated to be higher than those in Britain.

The effects of the worldwide recession beginning in 2007 hit Ireland as hard as they did any industrialised nation. However, after a difficult period of austerity, the country recovered well and is still in a strong economic position.

Today, Ireland is held up as a shining example of the benefits of entry into the EU. Control of public spending and investment in education since the 1950s created the right environment for the extraordinary turnaround in the country's fortunes. With its booming economy, a country that had been famous for mass emigration has become a magnet for immigrants.

Opposite: St Patrick's Day parade, Dublin.

Notwithstanding the Anglo-Irish Agreement, the violence in Northern Ireland continued throughout the 1980s. However, the main driver of the violence, the IRA, was beginning to be more political, largely because of its connection to the updated version of Sinn Féin. It was becoming increasingly clear to the IRA that their military campaign was not working and would not force Britain to leave Northern Ireland. In 1994, under pressure from the Irish and British governments and Sinn Féin, the IRA finally agreed to lay down its arms in order to negotiate a peace.

Four years of difficult multilateral peace talks produced the Belfast Agreement, signed by the United Kingdom and the Republic of Ireland on Good Friday, 10 April 1998. The Good Friday Agreement recognised that there would be no change to the constitutional status of Northern Ireland unless a majority of its citizens voted for it. The Republic of Ireland would amend its constitution to relinquish its territorial claim over the whole island of Ireland. Finally, it was agreed that only peaceful and democratic methods would be employed in the ongoing negotiations.

Less than two months later, the agreement was put to a vote in both Northern Ireland and the Republic. In Northern Ireland 72 per cent of those who voted supported the agreement, while in the Republic an incredible 94 per cent voted in favour.

On 2 December 1999, the Republic of Ireland amended its constitution, removing a major stumbling block to peace. The UK relinquished direct rule in Northern Ireland, and new agreements between the three parties to the agreement came into force. It was a first step, but an important one, towards peace in Northern Ireland.

Former Northern Ireland Secretary Mo Mowlam and artist Shane Cullen look at his work, *The Agreement*. The sculpture is 67 metres long and presents the 11,500 words of the Good Friday Agreement of 1998 mechanically inscribed onto 56 polyurethane panels.

The Government of Ireland Act 1920 established the Parliament of Northern Ireland as the devolved legislature for the province. It met at Stormont from 1922, and always had a Ulster Unionist Party (UUP) majority and administration. In 1972, with the situation in Northern Ireland deteriorating rapidly, the parliament was suspended and replaced with direct rule from Westminster. The short-lived Northern Ireland Assembly was established in 1973, but was brought down in 1974. Yet another Northern Ireland Assembly was set up in 1982, but without nationalist support it was dissolved in 1986.

Under the terms of the Good Friday Agreement, signed in April 1998, in November of that year the Northern Ireland (Elections) Act 1998 established the New Northern Ireland Assembly, with 108 members (MLAs), and the Northern Ireland Executive, a devolved, power-sharing executive led by a First Minister and Deputy First Minister, each with equal status, elected by the members of the Assembly.

The first election to the Assembly was on 25 June 1998, and it met on 1 July. Full powers devolved to it 18 months later, in December 1999. The first of six suspensions occurred just six weeks later. Initially, the Assembly had to suspend operations because of disagreements between the Unionist parties and Sinn Féin. The Unionists refused to participate until the IRA had disbanded and decommissioned its weapons.

The longest suspension of the Assembly, from October 2002 to May 2007, occurred when the Unionists withdrew from the Northern Ireland Executive. Eventually, after much negotiation, an election to the suspended Assembly was held on 7 March 2007. The DUP agreed to share power with Sinn Féin, and on 10 May, DUP leader Ian Paisley and Martin McGuinness of Sinn Féin took office as First Minister and Deputy First Minister. It was a historic moment, an unlikely cooperation between longtime foes, and it was the beginning of the longest unbroken period of devolved government, lasting until January 2017.

Ian Paisley (left), First Minister, and Martin McGuinness (right), Deputy First Minister, after being sworn in as Ministers of the Northern Ireland Assembly, 8 May 2007. They became known as the 'Chuckle Brothers'.

After the signing of the Good Friday Agreement in April 1998, it soon became clear, as had been feared and anticipated, that not all of the factions who had contributed to the violence of the Northern Ireland Troubles were happy with it.

On 15 August 1998, the town of Omagh in County Tyrone was blasted by a 227kg/500lb car bomb. It was a carnival week, and the town was crowded with shoppers and visitors. With 29 dead and around 200 injured, the enormous bomb blast was the deadliest incident of the entire period of the Troubles. The victims included Protestants, Catholics, teenagers, six children, a woman pregnant with twins and two Spanish tourists, members of a family visiting the town.

The bombing was claimed by the Real IRA, a splinter group who opposed the Good Friday Agreement and the IRA ceasefire that was a condition of the agreement. There had been a telephone warning, but the location of the bomb had not been specified, and police unwittingly moved the crowds towards the bomb rather than away from it. It was believed that the Real IRA had intended to bomb the courthouse (they said that they hadn't intended to target civilians), but the driver of the car couldn't find a parking space, and left the vehicle beside the busy market instead.

There was national and international condemnation. The atrocity could have put the peace process in jeopardy – instead it turned public opinion against the Real IRA. Sinn Féin's president, Gerry Adams, condemned the bombing in strong terms and the Real IRA apologised for the harm to civilians. In the wake of the bombing, the governments of Ireland and the UK enacted new anti-terrorism laws.

Perjury and poor police handling of the evidence meant that none of the convictions of those responsible stuck. The relatives of the victims campaigned long and hard for justice, which they achieved only in civil court, when four men were found liable for the attack and an award of £1.6 million in damages was made.

Omagh Bomb Memorial Gardens,
County Tyrone, Northern Ireland.

Although a separate Irish currency, which fluctuated in value against sterling, had existed during the 18th and early 19th centuries, the Act of Union in 1800 provided for the gradual assimilation of the Irish and UK pounds, a process that had been completed by 1828. Following independence in 1922, the Irish Free State introduced its own currency and coinage in 1928. The coins featured Ireland's native animals, with a Brian Boru harp on the obverse. The Free State pound maintained the link with sterling, pegged at a 1:1 ratio. In 1937, the state's name changed to Ireland, and the currency was known as the Irish pound. Ireland's external trade at the time was almost completely dominated by trade with Britain, so it made sense to maintain the link with sterling.

On Decimal Day, 15 February 1971, decimalisation of the currency was introduced in both jurisdictions. In Ireland it was overseen by the Irish Decimal Currency Board. At the same time the unquestioning acceptance of parity between sterling and the Irish pound was coming under the microscope. The 1970s was a period of high inflation in the UK and this was threatening to undermine Ireland's economic stability. In 1979, the European Monetary System (EMS) was established to promote closer monetary policy cooperation between members of the Economic Community (EC). Ireland joined the EMS, Britain didn't, and when sterling appreciated sharply, its link with the Irish pound, or 'punt', was broken.

The replacement of the Irish currency with the euro was initiated on 31 December 1998, when Ireland, together with 10 other EC member states, joined the Eurozone. The euro became Ireland's official currency for electronic transactions on 1 January 1999, but the five-week process of withdrawing Irish banknotes and coins from general circulation didn't begin until 1 January 2002. The transition to the euro marked a significant chapter in Ireland's economic history, giving it a hard currency and eliminating the need for currency exchange in trade with other Eurozone members.

'Crann an Óir' (Tree of Gold), outside the Central Bank of Ireland, Dublin.

From 21 to 29 July 2003, the island of Ireland hosted the 2003 edition of the Special Olympics World Summer Games, making it the first country outside the US to do so.

The seeds of the Games were planted in June 1963, when JFK's sister, Eunice Kennedy Shriver, set up a day camp, Camp Shriver, for children with intellectual disabilities. She had become aware that such children had few, if any, opportunities to participate in organised sporting events. The Kennedy Foundation went on to support dozens of similar camps throughout the US. Shriver then persuaded the Chicago park authority to join with the Kennedy Foundation in sponsoring a 'Special Olympics' in July 1968. The Special Olympics, incorporated later that year, provides training

for children and adults in more than 20 summer and winter Olympic Sports. In 1988 the IOC officially recognised the Special Olympics. There are editions of the Special Olympic Games every two years, alternating between summer and winter games.

In July 2003, around 7,000 athletes from more than 150 countries, supported by 30,000 volunteers, competed in the Dublin Special Olympics. Events were held in Dublin at Morton Stadium, the Royal Dublin Society (RDS) and the National Basketball Arena, and in Belfast at the King's Hall. The opening and closing ceremonies took place at Croke Park, although no events were held there. It was the first time the opening and closing ceremonies for the Special Olympics had been televised. The Games were opened by the President of Ireland, Mary McAleese. It was a star-studded event, and the impressive line-up of speakers included Nelson Mandela, who called the Games 'a testament to the indestructability of the human spirit', and Eunice Kennedy Shriver.

The 2003 Special Olympics World Summer Games, lobbied for by Ireland for five years, was transformational for the country. Taoiseach Bertie Ahern spoke of how people had been swept along by the magic of the Games, calling it 'one of our country's greatest achievements'.

Teams from around the world at the opening ceremony of the 2003 Special Olympics, at Croke Park stadium, Dublin.

When the IDA was formed in 1949 part of its brief was to stimulate foreign investment in Ireland. The first major tech company to set up an operation in Ireland was IBM, in 1956. The Lemass government's continuing drive to attract foreign investment during the first half of the 1960s led to Hewlett Packard, Microsoft, Dell, Oracle and Intel setting up Irish operations in the 1970s. The technology sector continued to grow exponentially – Google, Amazon and eBay, among others, arrived in Ireland in 2000, taking advantage of the tech-friendly environment created in the country.

Since the foundation of the state, education has been important, and there is now a heavy emphasis on STEM – the sciences, technology, engineering and maths. Courses in institutes of technology and universities attract overseas as well as Irish students, and the many graduates in these disciplines are an essential resource for the tech companies that have established themselves in the country. Opportunities in the industry include software development, data analytics, cloud computing and cybersecurity.

From its early beginnings in Ireland almost seven decades ago, the tech revolution has gathered pace, decade on decade and year on year. Ireland's favourable tax environment and young, highly educated English-speaking workforce have contributed to the country's emergence as a significant global player in the field of technology.

Ireland's EU membership and the trading opportunities associated with it have made it an attractive base for non-European companies looking for a trading platform to Europe. Dublin became home to the European headquarters of Google in 2003, followed by other major names, such as Facebook and Microsoft. The Apple headquarters are in Cork, where the company set up its Irish operation in 1980, just four years after it had been founded in the US. Ireland's rise as a tech hub is a testament to its strategic vision, investment in education and commitment to fostering innovation. Ireland is home to 16 of the top 20 global tech companies, employing more than 100,000 people.

As well as a headquarters building, Google was one of several companies that also offered subsidised housing in Dublin.

On 20 December 2004, the Northern Bank headquarters in Belfast was robbed of £26.5 million in cash. Sixty-three per cent of this was in uncirculated Northern Bank sterling banknotes, the remainder in used notes and other currencies. At the time, it was the largest bank robbery in UK history.

The robbery had been meticulously planned. On Sunday, 19 December 2004, the homes of two of the bank's employees, Chris Ward and Kevin McMullan, were invaded by armed men, who took Ward's family and McMullan's wife hostage. Ward and McMullan were told to turn up for work as usual the following morning, to fill a bag with £1 million in used notes and take it to a nearby bus stop as a trial run. They stayed in the bank after closing time, loading crates of banknotes onto trolleys and loading them into a van in the bullion bay. They then closed the bank and drove to Ward's house, where the men guarding

his family cleaned the house of any sign of their presence and left at 9.00 p.m. McMullan's wife, who had been taken from the family home, was released. As instructed, at 11.00 p.m., Ward called the police to notify them of the robbery.

The finger of blame was immediately pointed at the Provisional IRA, who issued a statement of denial a month later. There was a lot of speculation as to what the money was intended to be used for, arrests were made and charges brought, but no one was ever convicted of the robbery. Investigations turned up various amounts of the stolen banknotes in many different places, and there was a conviction for laundering some of the cash.

By March 2005, the bank had replaced the uncirculated banknotes with notes of different colours and serial numbers, so that any of the stolen notes would be difficult to spend. The £10 million in used notes and those issued by different banks were untraceable.

Police searching for evidence. Chris Ward was the only man charged with the robbery. He was found not guilty at a December 2004 trial.

Detective Superintendent Andy Sproule, outside Northern Bank headquarters in Belfast, with a replica of the white van used by the bank raiders in the multimillion-pound robbery.

Between 1987 and 2007 Ireland had gone from being one of the poorest EU member states to one of the most prosperous. The economy was growing at an average annual rate of 6 per cent. Big international firms, most of them American, were investing in the country.

Consumer confidence was high and credit was cheap, fuelling a boom in the building industry. People began to take on huge mortgages relative to their income. Between 1996 and 2006, property values quadrupled. Irish bank assets increased to five times the national GDP, based not on deposits but on the wholesale money markets.

When the effects of the 2007 global financial crisis began to manifest themselves, Irish property prices slowed down and the construction industry collapsed, leaving tens of thousands unemployed. Partly finished 'ghost estates' littered the countryside. Bank losses mounted. Overseas investment dried up. The government's tax take dropped by 20 per cent and welfare spending increased.

In 2008 the government guaranteed the liabilities of the major banks, nationalising two of them, and pouring €46 billion into them. It wasn't enough. Two years later, the banks were being kept afloat with emergency funds from the European Central Bank (ECB).

In 2010 the government secured €67.5 billion – 40 per cent of the Irish economy – over three years in loans from the EU and the International Monetary Fund (IMF). A 'troika' of experts was appointed to come up with a solution. Banks were merged and staff numbers reduced. A National Asset Management Agency (NAMA) was set up to recover large commercial loans. The nationalised banks went into liquidation. A new bankruptcy law was introduced to manage 100,000 private mortgage defaulters. VAT and carbon tax were increased and the Universal Social Charge (USC) on personal income was introduced. Welfare spending was protected, by and large.

By the end of 2012, the economy was recovering, unemployment began to reduce, and house prices began to recover as the country emerged from one of the most painful episodes in its history.

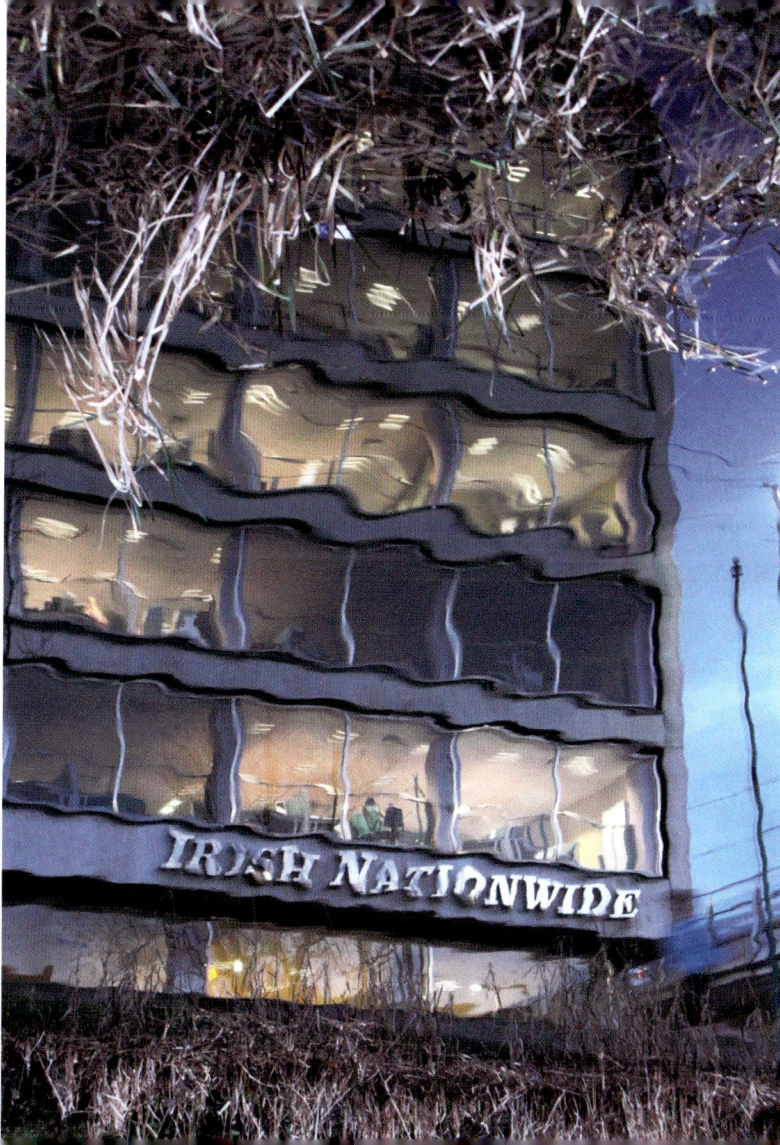

Irish Nationwide bank headquarters in Dublin reflected in the Grand Canal outside their office block. Irish Nationwide Building Society (INBS) played a role in the 2008 financial crisis by influencing other banks to lend too much money, which exposed them to the property market. When the financial crash occurred, INBS and Anglo-Irish Bank were among the first to fail, followed by other banks.

On 17 May 2011, Queen Elizabeth II arrived in Ireland at the beginning of a four-day state visit, the first by a British monarch since Irish independence. According to the Queen's grandson, William, Ireland was a room whose door had always been closed to her, and she was 'dying to see what's on the other side'. She had been invited by President Mary McAleese, and the visit was widely regarded as a normalisation of relations between the Republic of Ireland and the UK following the Good Friday Agreement in 1998 and the relinquishing by the Republic of its territorial claim to the whole island of Ireland. McAleese, countering objections to the visit, said that it was 'absolutely the right time' for the Queen to come to Ireland.

During her four-day visit, the Queen, known for her choice of colour to suit the occasion, wore various shades of green. Her carefully orchestrated schedule was packed. She laid a wreath at the Garden of Remembrance to honour those who died for Irish independence, then visited Trinity College Library to view the Book of Kells. The next day she visited the Guinness Storehouse and Government Buildings, laid a wreath at the National War Memorial Gardens, and then went on to Croke Park, site of the Bloody Sunday massacre in 1920. At a state dinner in Dublin Castle, she gave a speech on Irish–UK relations, which drew widespread acclaim. The following day she toured the Irish National Stud in County Kildare. On the final day she went to the Rock of Cashel, County Tipperary, en route to Cork, and the English Market. Her several public appearances had been at a distance, but in Cork she went on an unscheduled walkabout, greeting members of the public on the street.

Despite the naysayers, the Queen received an overwhelmingly positive reception. The Church of Ireland Archbishop of Armagh said afterwards that for most people 'it was time for this day, and they were glad to see it happen'.

A poster in Cork protesting
against the visit. There were
some anti-royal visit protests,
athough all were peaceful.

Queen Elizabeth II visits
the English Market in Cork
on 20 May 2011.

Index

Credits

The publisher gratefully acknowledges the following copyright holders. All images are copyright © individual rights holders unless stated otherwise. Every effort has been made to trace copyright holders, or copyright holders not mentioned here. If there have been any errors or omissions, the publisher would be happy to rectify this in any reprint. CC: Creative Commons.

3 Teapot Press
9 Teapot Press
11 Museo del Prado, Wikipedia/CC
20 Makasana Photo/Shutterstock
23 MNStudio/Shutterstock
27 Makasana Photo/Shutterstock
29 Teapot Press
30 Wikipedia/Isaacs Art Center
32 Teapot Press
33 Piotr Machowczyk/Shutterstock
34 Teapot Press
35 Borisb17/Shutterstock
36 Teapot Press
37 CPA Media Pte Ltd/Alamy Stock Photo
38 National Portrait Gallery, London
39 2024 Dean and Chapter of Westminster
40 National Portrait Gallery, London
40 Shutterstock
41 Nesbit1973/CC
43 Wikipedia/Internet Book Archive
44 CC
45 Teapot Press
46 Google Art Project
47 National Gallery of Ireland
48 Teapot Press
49 Mary Evans Picture Library
50 Benoit Daoust/Shutterstock
52 Courtesy of National Museums NI Ulster Museum Collection
53 Teapot Press
55 Richard J. King/Wikipedia/CC
56 Teapot Press
57 Belfast Harbour Commissioners/ Wikipedia/CC
58 National Portrait Gallery, London

60 National Library of Ireland
61 RobNaw/Shutterstock
63 Teapot Press
64 National Gallery of Ireland
66 National Gallery of Ireland
67 Chronicle/Alamy Stock Photo
68 Unknown
69 John Burns Library/Wikipedia/CC
70 National Gallery of Ireland
71 Plam Petrov/Shutterstock
72 Royal Museums of Fine Arts of Belgium/Wikipedia/CC
74 Irish Historic Houses
75 Wikipedia/CC
76 National Gallery of Ireland
77 National Gallery of Ireland
78 Yale Center for British Art/ Wikipedia/CC
79 National Gallery of Ireland
80 National Portrait Gallery, London
82 Library of Congress
83 Brest's Museum of Fine Arts/ Wikipedia/CC
84 Teapot Press
85 Teapot Press
86 Wikipedia/CC
87 Royal Collection
87 National Portrait Gallery, London
88 Teapot Press
89 Teapot Press
91 Teapot Press
92 Wikipedia/CC
93 Clare Library
94 Teapot Press
95 Wikipedia/CC
97 Artvee
99 IGHM, Quinnipiac University

100 Teapot Press
101 Everett Historical/ Shutterstock
102 Wikipedia/CC
103 US War Department, Office of the Chief Signal Officer.
104 The Irish Times
105 The Irish Times
106 National Gallery of Ireland
107 National Gallery of Ireland
108 Teapot Press
109 Library of Congress
110 Artvee
110 Wikipedia/CC
111 National Folklore Collection
112 Wellcome Images/CC
113 Teapot Press
114 Wikipedia/CC
115 Teapot Press
116 Top: Roma (née Bourke) O'Loughlin Family Collection
116 Wikipedia/CC
117 Pictorial Press Ltd/Alamy Stock Photo
118 National Portrait Gallery, London
119 Pictorial Press Ltd/Alamy Stock Photo
121 Wikipedia/CC
122 National Gallery of Ireland
123 Wikipedia/CC
124 National Gallery of Ireland
125 Wikipedia/CC
127 CC
127 CC
128 Wikipedia/CC
129 Teapot Press
131 RTÉ
132 Wikipedia/CC
132 Wikipedia/CC
133 Unknown

135 NLI/CC
137 NLI/CC
138 Wikipedia/CC
139 Wikipedia/CC
140 RAF Museum
141 Wikipedia/Derry Journal
141 Pictorial Press Ltd/Alamy Stock Photo
142 Alamy
143 Teapot Press
143 NLI/CC
145 PA Images/Alamy Stock Photo
146 Wikipedia/CC
147 Library of Congress
148 Wikipedia/CC
149 Wikipedia/CC
150 Cork City and County Archives Service
150 Teapot Press
151 NLI/CC
152 Wikipedia/CC
153 NLI/CC
154 Unknown
155 Wikipedia/CC
157 RTÉ
158 Reproduced courtesy of the RCSI
159 Unknown
159 LiamMurphyPics/Shutterstock
160 Wikipedia/CC
162 NLI/CC
163 Healy Limited Dublin/CC
164 Wikipedia/CC
165 Wikipedia/CC
166 Julian Herzog/CC
167 J Hinde / Mary Evans
168 Fine Gael/Wikipedia/CC
169 De Luan/Alamy Stock Photo
170 Chronicle/Alamy Stock Photo
173 ESB Archives/Wikiepdia

173 Ronin of Rock/Shutterstock
175 Unknown
177 Robert Ballagh, IVARO Dublin, 2024
179 Irish Photo Archive
180 Jonathan Ryan/CC
181 RTÉ
183 NARA/CC
184 NLI/CC
185 NLI/CC
187 RTÉ
189 Stephen Barnes/Northern Ireland/ Alamy Stock Photo
190 Teapot Press
191 European Communities/CC
193 Anwar Hussein/Alamy Stock Photo
195 Wikipedia/CC
195 Rob Bogaerts/CC
195 European Communities/CC
195 Nationaal Comité/CC
197 Trocaire/CC
199 PA Images/Alamy Stock Photo
200 Brendan Donnelly/Alamy Stock Photo
202 PA Images/Alamy Stock Photo
204 PA Images/Alamy Stock Photo
207 Ballygally View Images/Shutterstock
208 Stephen Barnes/Shutterstock
209 Shutterupeire/Shutterstock
210 PA Images/Alamy Stock Photo
213 Wirestock Creators/Shutterstock
214 PA Images/Alamy Stock Photo
215 PA Images/Alamy Stock Photo
217 Douglas O'Connor/Alamy Stock Photo
218 William Murphy/CC
219 Anwar Hussein/Alamy Stock Photo
Cover Teapot Press/Alamy/Teapot Press/ IGHM Quinnipiac University/Wikipedia CC/Teapot Press/Shutterstock/Teapot Press/Shutterstock

T154/1-25/01/TK1IB